CITY
PARKS

CITY PARKS

A stroll around the world's most beautiful public spaces

Christopher Beanland

BATSFORD

Opposite: Hyde Park, Sydney, Australia.

First published in the United Kingdom
in 2023 by
B. T. Batsford Ltd
43 Great Ormond Street
London
WC1N 3HZ

An imprint of B. T. Batsford Holdings Limited

ISBN 978 1 84994 768 8

A CIP catalogue record for this book is
available from the British Library.

10 9 8 7 6 5 4 3 2 1

Reproduction by Rival Colour Ltd, UK
Printed and bound by Vivar Printing Sdn,
Bhd., Malaysia

This book can be ordered direct from the
publisher at www.batsford.com, or try your
local bookshop.

CONTENTS

Introduction 6

UK and Ireland 18

Europe 54

Americas 98

Asia 132

Africa 172

Australasia 170

Index 204

Introduction

Play is the *sine qua non* of the park. This is the very quality missing from a modern life where we do too much, where we are too much. We sit and type, stand and talk, generate increasingly pointless plans and policies as the ecosystem collapses around us like a multistorey car park made of French toast, achieving nothing of note, scarcely dreaming. And all the while our egos balloon like a greedy uncle at Christmas, and our selfishness expands as capitalism caters to our every fleeting whim. We burn cash on crap and fry our eyes staring at screens and pour sawdust and glue into our cereal bowls because we're so tired. Even creatives who do have dreams end up running themselves into the ground, coughing up content to be packaged, streamed and consumed; they themselves consumed with their own *Torschlusspanik* at dusk when the work is not well received or – worse – never even greenlit. We're stuck on a treadmill. Some adults stretch out childhood well into their twenties, thirties or even forties, taking pleasure in life rather than sticking rigidly to the very Anglo and slightly sad *Brief Encounter* model of stolid devotion. You can see the trend: the Superdry dads at surf camps, buggering off to Sri Lanka, younger girlfriend in tow, fuelled on Huel. But mostly we fall in line – eventually – to be good consumers and hard workers, the American model gone mad.

Children act as a wake-up call, they make you realize that it's all as pointless as firing a pistol at an orange on a camel's head; life's travails will always be as increasingly bizarre as they are hard to get right. Kids focus the mind on the only thing that matters: people. And what's the best thing that people can do? Play. Have fun.

Take yourself back to your first memories. I'll bet a park figures, because the park is the first place we're taken out of the house to, it's the first in a series of adventures that get increasingly bananas through the teens and twenties, stopping off in bedrooms and at bonfires, in Croatia and Costa Rica, before existence goes grey and plateaus off into a weird simulacrum of what went before, to wit: marriage and our own parenthood, thence a comfy and steady decline hopefully marked by teas and not tears. We become our parents whether we want to or not, we become what we fear as teenagers, everything becomes the same. You instinctively want to give the gift of fun to kids like your parents gave it to you because fun softens the blows.

Hofgarten, Düsseldorf, Germany.

What is exciting in life is anything that is not the same. We cling on to that for a reason. Those first days out from the house in a pram, then a pushchair, then joyously and clumsily skipping, then on your bike with your first friends and scratched knees, each day more invigorating than the last, making sense of the world by experiencing and exploring elevates you. To learn things anew, as a child does, is to be freed from the quotidian prison of disappointment and sameness and to see everything with the brightness, contrast, volume turned up to max. This is what the park is about at a fundamental level: a way to experience urban life on a higher setting. The joyous abandon of the kids we see laughing so hard, with ice cream smeared around their greedy mouths, should be our impetus to remember the power of play and fun, its importance in our brief, flickering existences. And the park is where that force is deployed daily, in a safe and managed version of the almost-natural world where there are trees and shrubs but nothing that will hunt you, kill you and eat you (incidentally, one wonders whether this omnipresent natural danger is what slowly turned Australia into the biggest nanny state of all). And it's all completely free to the user – taxing local residents a small amount pays the costs of proffering paradise.

There are so many things we think we are that we are not. Life plays tricks on us. Romantic love is portrayed as altruism and snugs, and yet the reality is often a bleak zero-sum game where we are simply slaves to our own conscious and unconscious desires. This is not great for those of us who self-identify as romantics. To love is actually to want. Is it to care? We are fighting battles against our genes, against millions of years of evolution, against ourselves even – the book *Sex at Dawn* brings the sorry house of cards crashing down around us. Only therapy can fix this. What else? We are not natural home dwellers, we are not natural TV watchers, we are probably not even natural monogamous parents. We have become such strange creatures: technology has, more and more, bashed our brains as Ballard and Brooker predicted and yet we, despite our iPhone addictions, are so close to the foxes who scrabble around for the bones in fried chicken boxes, who follow you home, who you can almost talk to and feel such an affinity with on foggy 1am walks home, as Fleabag does. The truth is more brutal, as Werner Herzog reminds us: we are beasts. Animals who copulate indoors (the best thing that can be said for being inside, I guess). Animals are supposed to be outside. However, the many years we spent outside before architecture was 'a thing' has not disappeared from our synaptic receptors. It's still there. You only want to sit inside watching Netflix on cold Northern Hemisphere nights. But to be outside, well, that feels much more right.

Why do we dream of the mountains and the lake and the beach? Because we belong there, not on suburban housing estates, not in petit Parisian apartments where you can't swing un chat and you're f***ed if you fancy cooking up Pommes Anna on your one-ring hob. Housewives, shuttered in their kitchens, shunted to new towns or exurban estates in the middle of the 20th century, suffered depression. This is nothing new, women in a patriarchy will always suffer depression, but it showed us how wrong we were. We need people, communities and connections, to be listened to, not to work every hour that God sends, to remember to enjoy life like kids enjoy life, to grasp each second on this out-of-control, overheating rock hurtling through space as if it were our last, to go outside to the park and see the beauty in buttercups and daisy chains and playing tag or throwing a ball about, to stop and take a mental picture when we're picnicking with friends and realize that this is what human life is about – to be free, to be happy, to have fun, to be outside in the sun listening to Wet Leg on Spotify and the sound of the sparrows singing, to know that when the grisly and inevitable end comes it will have been a life, however short, well spent. Do not hesitate to skip lectures, to call in sick for meetings, to go and sunbathe in the park, to tell a person you are there with that you love them – and that you actually love them, you don't just want to possess them. Go and do some sport: jump in the lido, play tennis, get the cricket bat out of the cupboard, unpack the cornhole set and wonder what the f*** the rules are. Grab life by the lapels – it is short, all too short. Life feels real when lived in 3D, feeling the breeze and the hot sun, listening to shrill laughter and birds, tasting cold ice cream and tepid cava. This is not trite spin whipped up in the overcooled office of a lamentable 360 marketing agency on the Lower East Side; I'm telling you what the ingredients for a happy life actually are. But then you must ask yourself if you trust a writer; for we make the fake look real and sometimes the real look fake.

Like writing, city life is artifice, architecture is mostly a sham; to paraphrase my coolest politics lecturer Dr Ricardo Blaug: the whole world is a stage set that could collapse at any moment (as it has done to those unlucky enough to live in Ukraine, Syria, Ethiopia, Venezuela ...). People in the city are all social climbers – watch out. Are parks exactly what they promise us, or are they bullshitting too? Parks are not the beautiful wilderness that we really crave but nevertheless they will do the job of being a temporary sanctuary, just as we dream of a movie star but marry a mortgage advisor. We accept (some of us) that what's not quite perfect will be okay. Sold out of chocolate chip cookies? Get the hazelnut ones instead then. The realization that perfectionism will make you unhappy is an education that comes as one matures. The park gives us a taste of the natural world, a preened and primped world where the grass is cut and the flowers are arranged in some kind of crazy pattern. Herzog would never accept this distorted view of nature because it is too safe, too cultivated, totally inauthentic. Of course, the national park beats the city park just as the mountain lake beats the municipal lido, but one is a once-a-year treat, the other is there for us day in, day out. Yosemite, Death Valley, the Lake District – the dream of the Scottish naturalist John Muir brought to life in a way that emphasizes the white male predilection to own and dominate on one level and yet affords easy access to the beauty of the landscape for so many of us who love to walk the hills. But these landscapes too are built on the lies of *terra nullius*, and are faked and primped as well. The real countryside of farms and fields is often less pretty and less kind than city folk envisage (ask those who leave the city for the country what the reality is – no, the locals do not like Londoners, I'm sorry to break it to you). And country life itself is not like a glossy magazine despite what the travel industry wants you to believe. Yet ... for the majority of city dwellers around the world the fakeness of the nature in the national or local park is still okay, it will do.

Gardens are our own micro-version of this idea and loved, of course. How could you not relish a private outdoor sanctuary and the chance to watch your creations blossom and bloom? But they

Jardin des Tuileries, Paris, France.

themselves are even more of a fiction, a product of a disastrous suburbanization that has cost the planet dear by making us reliant on the car. Ian Nairn was right to lament the semidetsian suburbs. LA is as compelling as Reyner Banham showed us in his 1972 BBC travelogue, its pools especially define it; its garden-based urbanism comes at a high price though – air pollution and constant jams on Interstate 10.

Today's cities can't stop building parks. They began as municipal undertakings that were revolutionary. 'This could be my Hoover Dam,' says Amy Poehler in the always hilarious *Parks and Recreation*, when her city council clown Leslie Knope is proposing a new park on Lot 48. As with everything else that the modern era provided us with, and for which we're not grateful enough, parks were a plaything of the rich at first. As eventually bathrooms, decent housing *per se*, personal transport, good food and the rest of it trickled down from the powerful to the poor, so did parks. Aristocrats modelled the gardens of their stately homes after the enclosed hunting grounds that had for centuries allowed white men to do what they seemingly were unable to stop themselves doing: chasing animals and killing them. Many of both types – gardens and hunting grounds – became public parks as a sop to prevent the working classes from fully revolting: the former at Charlton, for example, and the latter at Hampton Court.

Paris's Jardin des Tuileries dates from the 1500s and Boston Common in the USA and London's Hyde Park from the 1600s. England was also where some of the first proper public parks were developed from scratch – Liverpool's Princes Park of 1842 and, across the Mersey, Birkenhead Park in 1847. Frederick Law Olmsted, the designer of New York's Central Park, visited Birkenhead Park and it's plain to see in the map of the park that its design – with lakes, ornamental structures, carriage drives, lawns and copses – looks strikingly similar to its Gotham cousin. Parks followed in all the great cities of the world, and then in virtually every town too. The Royal Parks of London, like Green Park, Greenwich Park and Richmond Park, were symbolic of a democratization of land, the first such move since enclosure had taken away common grazing rights and turned the world on its head in the Agricultural Revolution. Stately homes in the country would eventually almost always open their doors to the great unwashed, something unthinkable for centuries. Hyde Park was not unique in allowing free speech at Speakers' Corner, but it is the most famous example, where today a plethora of serious and bonkers views can be expressed.

It was the Industrial Revolution that brought the need for city and town parks to the fore. Mass migration had created urban areas that were not fit for purpose, people were living like rats in rookeries. Parks gave them air and space and the opportunity to play. If we think we work too much now (and we do, especially in America), look at how bad it was for Bradford's teenage wool factory inmates and Manchester's cotton brethren locked into a cycle of toil that Engels and Marx saw as the powder keg it so obviously was. Parks were humane, they gave us the chance to be human.

Modernism made us think more about health, the 20th century – the People's Century – brought sport to parks. Football, rugby and cricket stadia were built, cyclists appeared and, much later in the century, fun runners, and yoga practitioners and PTs with their high-paying victims wiggling arses as hard as teak. When I wrote my 2020 book *Lido* – about the history of outdoor swimming pools – I again ended up in many parks, because many parks were chosen as the perfect site for a pool: McCarran Park's pool in Brooklyn, Wycombe Rye Lido in High Wycombe's The Rye, London Fields and Brockwell and Parliament Hill Lidos on the edge of their respective London parks, the pool at Victoria Park in Sydney, Sommerbad Kreuzberg in Berlin's Böckler Park. The park and the lido go hand in hand: both signifiers of civic and personal virtue, both fun palaces, both codifying fresh air and exercise too.

As with lidos, parks were civic amenities that, it might be argued, worked best in a society where rules were followed, standards were strict and municipal beneficence was at its height. People parading around post-war parks in Sunday best while elaborate rose displays were carefully tended to was a symbol of a particular era. The dilapidated park peopled by dropouts, full of rubbish and crying out for horticultural attention is a 'sight-bite', as Jonathan Meades would say, from another era: from the 70s to the 90s when the park, like the city itself, was in a death spiral, when the Bronx was on fire and the pirate radio stations like Kool, Rush and Pure FM broadcast from the tower blocks of London's Nightingale Estate, their aerials overlooking Hackney Downs. Polite society was scared witless and people avoided Central Park and Tower Hamlets Cemetery after dark because of the violence. This gave outsiders their chance to colonize the space though: in came teenagers, skateboarders and anyone who basically had no cash. It was their chance to stamp their mark. Since the last century began parks have been on the rise, a trend inextricably linked to the growth in city living, gentrification and the rising value of land. More people of all stripes are living centrally and want access to these outdoor amenities,

councils are taking better care of their parks. The mosaic animals at Hackney Downs, in the shadow of the now low-rise Nightingale Estate and the private high rises that perversely followed, look beautifully cared for today. Some parks have always been rather better funded and looked after, for example the anomalous situation where the Corporation of London (rulers of the Square Mile) carefully and ambitiously manages green spaces far from the City, like Hampstead Heath, Queen's Park, West Ham Park, Highgate Wood and even Epping Forest – a sprawling woodland split into distinct sections, some of which are wild and some more like city parks.

Parks often have a memorial function. Death and nature go hand in hand – cemeteries memorialize the dead and Hiroshima's Memorial Park pays tribute to the atomic catastrophe which unleashed a tsunami of terror. Nature is about survival, about eating other life, about killing and procreating and ruthlessly spreading our genetic content in a way that we never really recognize or accept. We don't tell children about the reality of the situation, it is too upsetting. Anyway, we toughen up to get used to it, we want to protect our children from it and craft dreamy worlds where they can flourish away from the harshness. If only life was cute donkeys and pigs snuffling like on Hackney City Farm, next to Haggerston Park. If only industrialized food production and mechanized meat and fast food and all the horror had not stripped the Fens and the US Midwest and created monstrosities in the landscape – man makes things worse. Nature is brutal in a callous way, we are calculated – capitalism rides roughshod. However, we want to see the beauty in the natural world, perhaps our inclination is to see the best rather than the worst of something (or someone). We see in nature something redemptive. If man has made mistakes, can nature solve them? Today we lionize the natural world, we want to protect the environment (at least the young do – they will be inheriting a barely functioning Earth long after we who have seen so much have departed for nowhere else), sustainability and avoiding climate change is everything now, we hope that in saving the world we will save ourselves.

Nature is life too: the blooming roses symbolize another chance; the bees and the birds promise forgiveness and fruitfulness. Ultimately life and death are everything. One of them baffles us so we largely ignore it, the other is the driver for everything – sex, breeding, health, an aversion to danger. A fear of death and a lust for life drives us, that is innate. If you are the type of person who cultivates pothos and takes a particular pleasure in seeing it propagate you will probably make the best kind of parent to children. Gardeners and those that notice the plants in the park have a caring streak. When you hear a dad telling their daughter which tree is which or you see a tough council worker patiently tending to a border you see something beyond the brutality. It's the kindness and inquisitiveness that is also a part of being human, traits that are so attractive in others.

Cemeteries and parks have blurred boundaries. Bunhill Fields and the Glasgow Necropolis and Cimetière du Père Lachaise feel like parks, people use them as parks. It's interesting to note picnickers scoffing Scotch eggs next to Defoe's gravestone, lovers canoodling in thickets that look so haunted you would think twice about hanging out there after dark, people reading papers near the dead. The thick gothic woodland encasing the non-denominational graves at Abney Park Cemetery in Stoke Newington feels like the forest. The majestic views and open lawns on top of the hill at Glasgow Necropolis feel even more like a traditional Victorian park – it's a wonder you don't see more football being played. Benches are installed at regular parks to remind us of visitors who will visit no more. I read every inscription on every bench I sit on. When I see two names remembered together it tugs at the heartstrings. Isn't this a beautiful way to be remembered – together forever with your beloved, the two of you inspiring a new generation of writers to think about what real love, hard love, long-term love means, a love of sexual attraction but also of trust and care and dedication – and how when it ends in both of you going to wherever together, that situation does not leave one of you in an aching, impossible limbo. Even those memorialized alone on benches seem to have it good, remembered in their favourite park, sometimes along with their beloved dog who they used to walk there.

Parks should be for 'the people', right? Not all parks are public and the riff-raff was initially not wanted in these places of promenading. Although parks were 'for the people' they were actually, like council housing initially, 'for the right people'. The respectable working class could socially climb but those with braying dogs or children in rags were not tolerated. Private parks remain in many of London's 'Squares'. Ladbroke Square and Belgrave Square are open to residents only. Many have bitten the bullet and shinned over the rather large fence into Moseley Park in Birmingham, but the theory is that only residents can pay the annual key hire. The phenomenal success of the Open Garden Squares Weekend (and Open House) shows that a) we are nosey – and as a sometime journalist of course I empathize with this – and b) that we are besotted with plants and the outdoors. If we can't get in then it becomes even more attractive. Who has not wanted to see behind the walls of Buckingham Palace, just like when you were a kid and anything hidden behind a fence or a wall suddenly became the most exciting place in town? As with dating, what's not available to us takes on a strange lustre.

Although they look private, the City of London's gardens are small public parks which are some of the most charming additions to the Square Mile. The Salters' Garden in front of the brutalist Salters' Hall or the St Mary Aldermanbury Garden are oases during the week and practically deserted at the weekend, a real secret spot in London.

The rich have seized control now, pressing the 'Release the Hounds' button when they see the proletariat approach; private has pulled the rug from public, or – as Anna Minton helped to explain – there really is no new public space any more, the creep of the market is almost total. Yes, Manchester has the first new park in its city centre for a century near to Piccadilly Station, but, as the website explains in an unselfconsciously Orwellian way: 'To keep the park clean, well maintained, curated, impressive and secure 24 hours a day, 365 days a year, it will be a privately managed estate under single private ownership.'

Parks illuminate the fundamental unfairness at the bitter heart of the system we never question because we're not supposed to. Of course we must. Nietzsche: 'The philosopher has to be the bad conscience of his time; for that purpose he must possess its best knowledge.' That inequality of access is all the more stupid when Kevin Cahill reminds us that – even looking ahead to 2050 when the population will be higher – the world's 37 billion acres of land means that every single person could have four acres of their own. They do not and they will not. Instead, a few own almost everything, leaving everyone else owning almost nothing. Do we give a shit? Apparently not. This undemocratic access to land at every scale means you're lucky to get a garden, in fact you're lucky in some countries to even get the most basic flat to dwell in. Real-estate prices have spiralled out of control against incomes. Property, along with – perhaps – Bitcoin, as Max Keiser *et al* suggests, seems a rare safe hedge as economic Armageddon rolls on. Quantitative easing means money becomes slowly worthless as the Fed simply prints billions more dollars. A clear line is drawn between owners and renters and the end result is human tragedy on a massive scale, as Vicky Spratt points out in her book *Tenants*.

Finsbury Park and Clissold Park in London were supposed to have been developed for housing in the 1800s but were saved for the people. The park becomes an absolute essential function of a democracy and is almost radical if you think about how much speculators would make from real estate if we were to hypothetically demolish Hyde Park and Central Park and build on the most expensive land in the world. This will never happen, yet corners of parks are chopped off and built on; from highways to hotels – the green lungs are eroded.

New parks keep arriving though – so many of them it's almost impossible to keep up. There are stylistic exercises like Zaha Hadid Architects' new park at Eleftheria Square in Nicosia, Cyprus, or 'greenways' like Cardiff's forthcoming Gateway

Eleftheria Square, Nicosia, Cyprus.

Linear Park. Often the developments are on a smaller scale. Tiny pocket parks pop up across Japan, Boston's waterfront has new skinny linear parks. In London streets swap car parking for parks, with the parklet concept spreading across two-car bays, as in San Francisco and other cities. The one in Princess May Road, Dalston, was particularly pleasing. The Colvestone Crescent one on the road on which I used to live a very happy life brought residents together. Chairs, planters, toys, a table, all perched on a basic wooden structure – the anti-High Line, really. Community-focused, cheap, extremely popular in summer and a way to bring neighbours together who don't have much in common in this atomized world except sharing gossip and moaning about bin collections on nextdoor.com. The Guerrilla Gardeners of Manchester, Detroit and Copenhagen have taken radical action by cultivating land next to roads and on abandoned lots, for food or fun. Bold actions like these are aimed at combatting the dominance of cars, the concentration of land with the few, the concreting of everything. But what's interesting is how much of our cities could become a park. The more you look the more you see unused land everywhere. Turning much of this wasted space into a park would require just a bit of effort. But look again and you also see plenty of green space ready to be used too. Grass next to roundabouts, in front of tower blocks, by retail parks, between railway tracks, along riverbanks. None of it really being used. As with fashion, it takes one person to go and sit there before the many follow. But, as with politics, once a few are there, there is no stopping the movement. A little effort and imagination could turn these 'in between' green spaces into thriving new parks. And what about roof parks atop every building, or school

playing fields opened every weekend? There's no end to the possibilities of how we can green our cities and improve access to open space.

In today's super-sexualized, crassly consumerist society where everyone seems to be competing – whether it's on Hinge or for housing – spectacle is everything. Everyone is selling something, from themselves to their ideas. Social media is a ridiculous circus of onanistic one-upmanship, TikTok dances have usurped Derrida, our every fruitless move in life's chess game has become performative as we are all bashed over the head again and again by a metaphorical rubber mallet as if on children's TV. Dating has never been more about peacocking, fame becomes the goal by default, altruism and patience are swilled down the drain, consumption of experiences seems like one of the few acts of self-succour we have left as the money drains away and the forests slowly smoulder. Writing a book is not enough: it has to be flogged on telly and at talks to an overstimulated audience whose attention span is being squished with a potato masher. I'll be reading this bit out at a talk soon, dear reader; please laugh at the meta insanity of it all ...

Is it any wonder that urbanism has felt the need to fiddle on a grand scale while Rome burns? Increasingly shit, showy ideas have gained traction. Thankfully those of us still with eyes propped open like Alex in *A Clockwork Orange*, traumatized but still willing to radically observe as the last revolutionary act left to us, can see the sham. The curtains have been pulled back and the levers revealed. With the case of the widely ridiculed Marble Arch Mound – a £6 million Toblerone piece of highly unnatural materials coated in the thinnest layer of grass – it was not so much seeing how the sausage is made as being invited by the farmer to pull the trigger on the captive bolt gun yourself. Bye-bye, Babe.

Skive off, say no to grafting, join everyone else in the park. London Fields on an August afternoon is hilarious, so full of people who've jacked in work, who've got off the treadmill. Matt Haig says: 'To be calm becomes a kind of revolutionary act.' In this case calmness comes primarily from being outside, on the grass, beneath the blue skies and the starlings, next to the ants who crawl over your hand. Because, as screwed as modern society is, we can find easy ways to rebel against it at a micro level and to thrive in the cheap peace and pleasure still available to us. If to be calm is a revolutionary act then to go to the park and kick a football and climb a tree and plant a bush and walk a tightrope and laugh with your friends and family and lover are all revolutionary acts too. Imagine if we all downed tools, if we all threw a million Android phones in the Serpentine, if we stripped off our stupid clothes and just chilled in the majesty of the sunny present. Throw this book down, which itself was written partly in parks on sunny arvos, get on your bike, go and walk, purchase an ice cream, enjoy the crispness of the cold on your face if it's winter; strip off and bake in the sun if it's summer. The park is everyday and unremarkable, yet it is also a special place where urban society can congregate and individuals can find their own space. It is a *memento mori* of somewhere we can never return to and yet long for: our childhoods and our agrarian and rural pasts. We revel in the park's space, in its approximation of nature, in its atmosphere of freedom. It is life and death, everything and nothing; it is where memories are made and the in-between days when nothing happens.

I searched in vain for the elemental essence of what needed to be said and it came to me right at the end of the writing process, the night before deadline day. I spent the end of May 2022 walking through LA, to plush Barnsdall Art Park with its Frank Lloyd Wright house for Alice Barnsdall and chilling hipsters, and to the top of the mountain on which the Hollywood sign sits above Griffith Park, and I finished in the wild post-modernism of Pershing Square. On this last night I realized that the writer's real duty is to explore and explain, to observe and immerse and discuss everything from the luxurious to the ludicrous. In Pershing Square homeless Angelinos slept and in the Skid Row streets nearby that stank of piss thousands more milled like zombies, so removed from the glitz of the most glamorous city on Earth. Cyclists yelled in Spanish, people sported outlandish outfits, oblivious cop cars cruised by. I bought a pizza slice and stood on a sketchier corner. A guy called Stacey appeared as if from the pages of a screenplay and told me he'd served 17 years in a supermax for three minor crimes and that books kept him going. He couldn't remember the name of one in particular, but it taught him, he said, that 'life was all about energy and balance'. That is the answer: writers must show us the breadth of worlds and parks are the parts of cities where you can really see this breadth on show: each park has a different feel but all of life's beauty and ugliness plays out in them, all of its energy and balance. They are the most perfect places to revel in humanity's contradictions. I finished writing and looked forward to poring over the edits while I sat in the park. We need the park; it needs us too.

UK AND IRELAND

VICTORIA PARK

London

On cold days and warm days alike I've
donated hours of a life which ultimately will
be too short to Victoria Park. I've talked
shop, flirted, dated, complained, felt elated,
learned exercises, biked, picnicked, laid
on the ground next to people I care about
and watched the clouds and the starlings
flit across the sky. I've dreamed, planned,
wondered, wished things would happen the
way I needed them to, felt excited, compelled,
downcast. In lockdown, when things were
always awful, and in the sunny times before
the nightmares of 2020 began, the park was
for me, like so many others, a place where
all different kinds of life revealed themselves.
Why is it so popular? This People's Park was
always a democratic undertaking, near to
so many people who have regular lives and
incomes. Shaped like a Wellington boot
and wedged between two canals and some
gorgeous housing, the park was a marvel of
Victorian benevolence. Its Chinese Pagoda
was thought of as wildly exotic, it had a lido
until 1990 – now is the time to rebuild. It has
cafés and pubs on its outskirts. It is guarded by
two Dogs of Alcibiades at the Bonner Street
entrance – marble sculptures of Molossian
Hounds donated by Lady Regnart in 1912. And
in summer it is a perpetual haven. It's even the
venue for various music festivals. The park has
recently come to prominence again due to
Gemma Reeves' eponymous novel about the
people who live around its edges.

THE WALKS

King's Lynn

A perfect example of a small-town park that's been lovingly restored (in this case in 2007) after decades of being rather dilapidated. When I was walking through here with a girl from school I fancied (and won't name to save her embarrassment) and asked her out halfway down St John's Walk in 1997 (she said a polite 'no') it was looking rather tired. When I joined my parents for a festive stroll on Christmas Day 2021 the park was looking up. The handsome Victorian bandstand on an island surrounded by a moat from the diverted Gaywood River is a nice touch; so is the town wall, gates and 15th-century Red Mount Chapel built for pilgrims en route to Walsingham. All of which has gained The Walks a Grade II listing from Historic England for its long history and unusual combination of landscapes and buildings. There's even The Walks football stadium, home to the plucky 'Linnets' – King's Lynn Town FC.

WOODHOUSE MOOR

Leeds

A tonic for generations of Leeds University students (myself included), Woodhouse Moor's windswept uplands sit high on a hill and feel slightly wild. In summer, parties and picnics and sports dominate; during the less warm weather (of which Leeds has more than its fair share) you can spot other things in the park, like the statues of dignitaries, always with traffic cones on their heads, and the gardeners toiling at the allotments. Sometimes students call it Hyde Park, which is not hugely surprising really, as the park's official branding is pretty minimal and there's a big traffic junction at the northern edge called Hyde Park Corner. All the streets overlooking the park are almost entirely student rentals and if you can get a place on Hyde Park Road overlooking the lawns you know you've made it in student digs-ville. I don't know why, but food remains my overriding memory of Woodhouse Moor: curries at Akmal's – the former toilet block in the trees which is now a popular student tandoori venue – and four-cheeses pizzas from Lucky's, which overlooks the park. I always remember walking through the park every day to my own student house down the hill in Burley Park and watching American post-rock bands like June of 44 in The Library pub by the southern corner of the park.

BOTANIC
GARDENS

Belfast

Presided over by two very different buildings,
Belfast's Botanic Gardens is as much of a treat
as a bag of cheese and onion Tayto crisps.
On one side sits the Ulster Museum, with its
radical 1972 brutalist extension by Francis Pym,
an aggressive gesture built during the most
aggressive period in the province's history. To
the north lies the monumental Palm House of
Charles Lanyon's design, dating from 1840.
Inside this steamy, tropical greenhouse you
can find all sorts of exotic delights, like the
globe spear lily. The park sits next to Queen's
University and even has its own station,
Botanic, on the Northern Ireland rail network.

PHOENIX PARK

Dublin

If you want to talk about size then Phoenix Park is a clear winner – Europe's largest enclosed city park boasts 700 hectares of space. So there's a lot going on here in the west of Dublin. The Wellington Monument towers over the oaks and grass. The residences of the American Ambassador and the Irish President sit in the park – and they're not the only ones living here, there are thousands of deer which have become symbols of the park. Streams and lakes criss-cross the park too and in summer there are numerous concerts here: Arcade Fire and Kanye West have kept tipsy punters happy (not at the same time though).

Parks and Photography

James Drury
Photographer

What do you love about photographing parks?

I love photographing parks because there's always something that captures my eye, even if I've been to the same place hundreds of times. The light looks different every time you go there; the landscape changes with the seasons; there are different people; sometimes I'll find a city of spiders' webs strung up in a big patch of otherwise unattractive scrub; or someone's hung something from a tree. What attracts me to parks – particularly ones in cities – is they're so democratic. The park is where everyone goes, like some kind of enormous communal back garden. So you'll find people sunbathing, walking their dog, exercising, meeting friends, picnicking, doing a hobby ... I like people-watching and parks are perfect places to do that.

Why do parks make for good photos?

Parks make good photos for all the above reasons, but also simply because they're a space where the natural world is accessible. People are drawn to nature – there's something primal, soothing, uplifting about it, whether you're looking at a stunning landscape or closely inspecting an unfurling leaf bud.

We've been on lots of walks across Wanstead Flats with Toby your dog – what do you like about this place in particular?

Firstly, Wanstead Flats and Wanstead Park are my closest bits of green space, so they're most convenient. But the fact that the flats are – well, flat – means you get stunning sunrises across the football pitches. There's also plenty of ponds and lakes which have interesting wildlife around them, and there's a really interesting history to them, stretching right back to when it was a royal forest. You can still see leftover relics from the Second World War here, such as the foundations of a Nissen hut and what I think are tethers for barrage balloons.

Which other parks do you like to explore and photograph?

I love cities, and when I travel to other places I always make sure I visit parks. Letna Gardens in Prague is a favourite. Located high on one of the hills, it has the obvious attraction of views over the city below, but there's also an enormous metronome on the site of where a statue of Joseph Stalin used to stand. It also has a great beer garden. In Tokyo, there are some stunning traditional Japanese landscaped gardens, but I love Yoyogi Park, which is less intricate but is amazing for seeing the city have fun and relax. Tokyoites head here to meet up and share their passions – you'll see groups of rockabilly enthusiasts, jugglers, skateboarders, goths, and they all occupy little clusters. And in autumn the gingko trees are unmissable. If you're in New York, forget Central Park – Prospect Park in Brooklyn is way better. It's so varied. You can meander among quiet trees, or explore the formal Japanese Hill and Pond Garden, walk around the lake, or an 18th-century farmhouse, which houses an interesting museum about the area. The Carousel

is good for cheesy but colourful photos, especially at dusk. Victoria Park is the best park in London and if you don't agree, we can't be friends.

What are some memories you have of being in parks – as a kid and as an adult going to festivals, etc.?

My earliest memory of being in the park was with my parents in Leamington Spa – I think it must have been Jephson Gardens – and I vividly remember seeing landscapes I'd never encountered before. I found them fascinating. Since then, I've had your typical teenage underage-drinking-in-the-local-park shenanigans, including being sat around with some cider, mates and a battery-powered radio when we found out who had won the chart battle between Blur and Oasis (I wanted Oasis to win at the time because Blur were 'too poppy', so I was bitterly disappointed, but ended up being an enthusiastic convert to the Essex band a year later). As a young adult, I found myself writing more about parks than visiting them – I was a local newspaper journalist so would cover controversies over plans to build housing, or (more often than not) the continual blight of dog poo. But moving to London when I was 26, I found myself able to spend more time in parks – there are so many here and they're the perfect place to get together with friends when the weather is good. And sometimes even when it's not.

SUTTON PARK

Birmingham

Teenage memories for many Brits of a certain age include a summer pilgrimage to the BBC Radio 1 Roadshow. Crucially it was free (we were skint) and featured a host of pop acts of the moment with all manner of creepy and/or cool DJs introducing. The Roadshows pitched up at parks in seaside resorts and small towns, and in 1992 the largest ever hit Sutton Park to celebrate the station's 25th anniversary, with Aswad and Del Amitri playing. And in 2004 the rebooted version, One Big Weekend, took over Perry Park, just down the road. I was there in 04 watching Razorlight, Kasabian and The Departure. One wonders what Henry VIII would have made of it all – he gifted the former royal hunting park at Sutton, which is larger than the town next door, to its people. Sutton Park's most alluring asset is the mainline goods railway that unusually stretches out down its length and provides much amusement to kids. They will also love the donkey sanctuary and activity centre. There was a lido here until 2003 – and if you're listening, Birmingham City Council, it's high time to get it reopened. In the absence of the lido there are still plenty of ponds to explore.

HOLYROOD PARK AND ARTHUR'S SEAT

Edinburgh

Holyrood is an extremely unlikely example of a mountainous park within a city. Were it not for the thousands of others who will also join you on this odyssey through Edinburgh's wildest and windiest slice of land, you'd almost believe you were in the Highlands. The extinct volcano of Arthur's Seat broods over the Scottish capital, whose dour architectural heft seems to honour the greyness of the mountain and Salisbury Crags. At the foot of the hill you can find the Scottish Parliament, while in the park itself there are colonies of fulmars and stonechats, and hares and orchids can also be found. During Festival season you'll spy narcissistic hungover stand-up comics and over-exuberant experimental student-theatre practitioners slogging up to the top of Arthur's Seat, ciggies and vodka in hand, heads full of dreams of stardom and success.

HAMPSTEAD HEATH AND PRIMROSE HILL

London

Two of London's nicest places to live – Hampstead and Primrose Hill – also have the city's nicest parks. I used to live in a scruffier neighbourhood between the two but I took up jogging to get over a break-up in 2008 and found both were perfect for blowing away the cobwebs. I'd blast up to the summit of each park in turn (Parliament Hill, Primrose Hill Summit) while listening to Ben Folds Five. I began to feel like I wasn't the only one because these parks are always crawling with runners. 'The Heath', as Londoners know it, is so big and so wild it doesn't so much feel like a park as being out in the countryside of Surrey or Hertfordshire. Owned and run by the City of London, it features huge expanses of gorse and grass and pretty steep inclines and cycling bans. One of the hidden wonders of the Heath is the Hill Garden and Pergola, an atmospheric and often deserted Georgian terraced garden with a big pergola. Primrose Hill is smaller and is managed alongside the next-door Regent's Park by the Royal Parks. Like Parliament Hill, you get views over Central London's skyscrapers that the entrepreneurial would consider charging for. These vistas mean both spots are perfect for getting smashed at sunset. Sledgers will always try their luck on Primrose Hill on the rare occasions London gets snow, and in both parks you can observe the super-rich and celebrities out for a promenade.

CRYSTAL PALACE PARK

London

The highlight of any visit to Crystal Palace Park is the sculptures of dinosaurs that don't look exactly like the real thing but are almost good enough to convince kids that this is what dinosaurs look like. A real feat of Victorian bravado from an age where everyone was drunk all the time and yet anything was possible. The natural world was being relentlessly studied, mapped and, of course, shot dead in the name of science. So here we have a collection of slightly woozy and sleepy Iguanodon, Teleosaurus, Megalosaurus and the rest frozen mid-clamber on an island in a lake. They were the perfect accompaniment for something else out of this world – Joseph Paxton's Crystal Palace. The glass palace showcased booty, biology, engineering, art and ideas from around the British Empire. It began life in another park – Hyde Park, in 1851, site of the Great Exhibition. It came to south London in 1854, giving its name to the park, suburb and football team. The palace stood proud until being ravaged by flames in 1936. Though in an interesting footnote, various plans have been put forward for it to be rebuilt here. The park was also used for other events – the 1911 Festival of Empire and numerous athletics, football and motor speedway competitions. There's also a large maze. Another attraction is the beautiful Victorian railway station and the Italianate subway/arcade linking it to the park, which is one of the most popular 'hidden' sights of London.

Garden Festivals

If the great post-war Expos in Brussels, Seattle, Montreal and Osaka and the World's Fairs held in New York essentially softened up the general public to the oncoming onslaught of modern architecture (modern architecture did not last very long in the grand scheme of things though), then the garden festivals that came after perhaps prepared us for a new era of eco-consciousness and dendrophilia. Soon we would all be tree-huggers, we would all have sap in our veins and eyes lasering in on lilies.

What's often forgotten in the concrete-drenched rhetoric of those slightly earlier times is that the modernists actually wanted to create a world where parks, gardens and green space' were there for everyone. That story has been lost somewhat. Tower blocks didn't come with intentionally dumped Tesco trolleys and grimy gravel next to them, this was supposed to be space to play, relax and enjoy the outdoors.

Nevertheless, as the modernist architectural icons have fallen like so many dominoes, the popularity of parks and gardens has risen. We've learned to love the outdoors and care for it more too. Remember the 'Gold Violin' episode of Mad Men where Betty dumps all the waste from a picnic on the grass and Don throws a spent beer can after it before driving away? We seem to have moved into a different era where

The Homebase Urban Retreat garden at the 2015 Chelsea Flower Show, London, UK.

FESTIVAL GUIDE

Opens 10 am Daily

International Garden Festival
LIVERPOOL '84
2nd May to 14th October

£1.50

Guidebook, International Garden Festival 1984, Liverpool, UK.

protecting the environment has become front and centre, and enjoying parks and gardens is part of that.

The garden festivals were there to show us how to plant more exciting back yards than just grass and a pathway. But what they actually resembled were giant, vibrant city parks filled with various fun rides and attractions as well as overblown displays of tulips spelling out words and esoteric ways of displaying plants (plus, naturally, lots of water gardens). And they proved phenomenally popular. Not just with gardening mums either, but everyone.

The 1988 Glasgow Garden Festival drew almost 5 million to the banks of the Clyde – even The Proclaimers can't do numbers like that. They came to see what was more like a funfair in some respects. This festival, and the 1984 one in Liverpool, had something in common – they were both trying to kick-start the regeneration of brownfield industrial sites next to previously teeming rivers, an attempt to rebrand a post-industrial Britain that was also seeing the en masse roll-out of B&Qs and Do It Alls on out-of-town trading estates catering to those with new suburban houses and gardens and green fingers. Gateshead followed in 1990 and Ebbw Vale in 1992 – again, struggling post-industrial locations the Tories had screwed and then tried to save. The Liverpool festival even featured a Japanese Garden and a miniature railway, and – naturally – Beatles-themed floral displays.

The garden festival idea can be traced back to the germ of the Chelsea

Flower Show, the Royal Horticultural Society's annual spring showcase that began in an earlier form way back in the 1860s, when city parks were also beginning to roll out. In Britain, the garden festivals were tied to a Thatcherism mired in anti-modernism, suburbanization and middle-class-ization, and were needed in a way precisely because government policy took away the industrial (and, ergo, political) might of these former solidly working-class coal, steel and ship-building areas. Yet they presented a green-fingered vision of a different way forward that would be less harsh, perhaps.

The idea has spread worldwide. Garden festivals have happened in Antalya, Beijing, Chiang Mai, Kunming, Osaka, Vienna, Singapore, Taipei, Melbourne, Taichung, Yangzhou, Qingdao and Dijon. The Netherlands and Germany were pioneers in these festivals. Holland has hosted many huge garden festivals – the 'Floriade' has come to Rotterdam, Amsterdam, Venlo and The Hague. In summer 2022 it rocked up at Almere, though there was speculation it could be the last. Germany has also hosted major international garden festivals at Stuttgart, Rostock, Munich and Hamburg; the 2027 iteration will come to the post-industrial Ruhr Valley. This is in addition to the biennial Bundesgartenschau, which takes place at different cities around the country. In 2023 Doha hosts a garden festival under the Qatari sun – an intriguing proposition in this desert city.

Bundesgartenschau, Heilbronn, Germany.

WELLNESS

Samantha Lewis
Wellness journalist

What do you love about exercising in parks?

I love exercising in parks as I crave peace and quiet and
the space to move freely. It's something I do less of in
winter when you risk losing a toe to frostbite, but come
summer I'm all for exercising in the great outdoors.

Why makes parks so good for wellness?

Exercising in parks has many benefits for your body and mind.
It has been shown to lower stress, regulate sleep, boost vitamin
D levels and enhance overall mood. In fact, research suggests
spending just 20 minutes in a park is enough to improve wellbeing.

Which parks are great for yoga and why?

All parks! The wonderful thing about yoga is you can do it
anywhere. Practising among nature helps to ground you, which is
a huge part of yoga. It also brings enhanced focus as the grassy
surface requires you to work harder, especially in balancing poses.

Which park do you like to exercise in?

Finsbury Park in London is my nearest green space and I'll head there a few times a week to do a walking meditation. This involves walking slowly, breathing in fresh air and tuning into my surroundings. The park also has a great outdoor calisthenic gym if you enjoy bodyweight training.

What are some memories you have of being in parks?

My most vivid memory is visiting Central Park in New York on a freezing cold day in November. I was in total awe of the park's beauty – all fiery orange and yellow with a backdrop of Manhattan skyscrapers. I lingered by Wollman Rink, watching people ice skate while warming myself with hot chocolate. I think it's when my crush on the city began.

Can you tell us more about parks and wellness?

Interestingly, the Japanese are world leaders when it comes to green spaces and wellness. The now trendy term 'forest bathing', or *shinrin-yoku*, was coined in Japan in the 1980s. It became a public health initiative aimed at stressed-out urbanites after the government researched the benefits of spending time among trees.

EUROPE

PARQUE EDUARDO VII

Lisbon, Portugal

The Estufa Fria is a hidden delight in chaotic Lisbon. This botanical garden complex takes visitors around a world of plants. I pass by cacti and calathea, and even chickens and baby coots, in search of an oddity. In 2020, Belgian artist Nicolas Lamas tried to install his sculpture *Illusion of Stability* here. It mused on man's existential flimsiness, the fact that we can't control the world the way we think we can. It was to prove apt. The technology-filled work was destroyed by a storm before it could be unveiled. A marker, crouching between some ferns, tells the story of this fascinating scenario. The poignancy of the whole enterprise would not be lost on anyone who thinks about the planet as an integrated system and it certainly wasn't lost on Lisbon, which was 2020's European Green Capital. The Estufa Fria, a fascinating confection of greenery, lakes and odd architecture, has been caring for the world and its plants for hundreds of years. It is the main attraction of Eduardo VII Park, which is being nicely restored; it is the city's lungs. It was renamed in 1903 for the British king in honour of the centuries-old Anglo-Portuguese alliance – the world's longest. The park offers cracking views over Lisbon, a tennis centre and interesting formal hedge planting. It was redesigned in the Salazar era and includes some fascistic triumphal columns. Cross the new pedestrian bridge at the northern end to see the fascinating brutalist Palace of Justice building.

TEMPELHOF

Berlin, Germany

The heft of the Zentralflughafen terminal at Tempelhof is the setting for such real-world shindigs as the Berlin Festival (where the former business lounge became the VIP party room) and the fictional undertakings in DBC Pierre's disgustingly prescient *Lights Out in Wonderland* (someone please make a film of this book). Supposedly detoxified from its Nazi architectural origins, the redundant airport – in addition to hosting numerous events and latterly asylum seekers on its apron – is also one of Berlin's biggest parks. The novelty of being able to walk the taxiways and runways fulfils a fantasy that many of us have had when staring from the windows of a 737 – to be able to get out and fully explore the airport on foot. Here you can do just that, taking in control towers and radar boxes, railway tracks and tarmac. Skaters (and wind skaters) and cyclists and kids are especially fond of this place. I love the old Dakota aircraft parked around that remind you of the Berlin Airlift (see more photos of that at Tempelhof S-Bahn Station). Down at the end of Runway 09R one summer's day, watching the long grass and buttercups ping in the breeze, I remember another fantasy unfurling – what if a plane landed here right now. It did, once – in 2010 a pilot performed an emergency landing in his single-seat prop trainer. Footnote: now Tegel is also closed, Berlin will soon have another park on the site of a former airport.

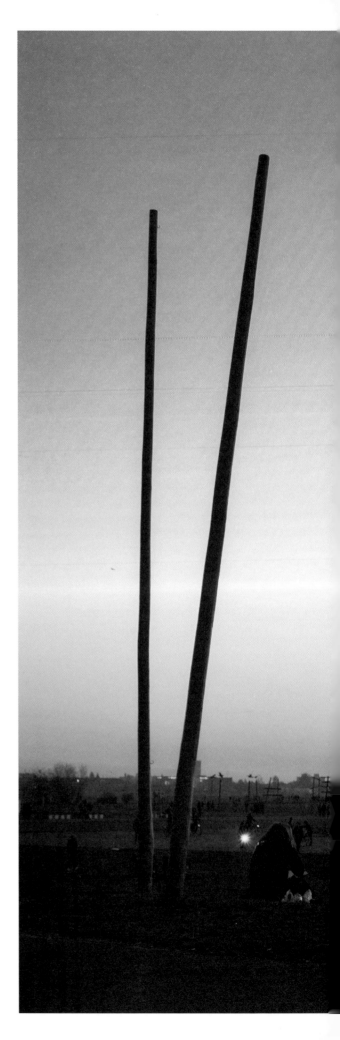

PARK GÜELL

Barcelona, Spain

Funny how some parks become de facto tourist attractions (the High Line being the most obvious example) and here in Barcelona the story is no different. This is not, of course, a place to come in search of solitude and you won't find many locals relaxing as with a usual park. Instead, visitors cram in to see Gaudí's flamboyant and playful buildings and other touches: the mosaic salamander that you might be forgiven for thinking was designed specifically by Gaudí to be a background to Instagram selfies, and the curving serpentine benches, as well as the uniquely exuberant houses and planting terraces. Whenever I've been here it's been hotter than the inside of an apple pie. You always seem to need a sit-down after the schlep up from the nearest station, which seems to involve walking along too many main roads. The origins of the park are wrapped around Gaudí's commission from Eusebi Güell to design a place for people to play and actually to live too. Some of the designs were also by Josep Maria Jujol. The views belong to the city and are wonderful: the Modernisme district unfurls in front of you until your eye reaches the cool, calm sea in the distance.

PARC DE LA VILLETTE

Paris, France

Don't ask me why, but one too many romantic adventures to Paris have ended in unmitigated disaster. Perhaps the city of love is too much; better to try your luck in Hunstanton? The one time things did go like *le mouvement d'horloge* we strolled up the Canal de l'Ourcq in the sun, past hipster cafés, and found ourselves in Paris's philosophical park set on their former abattoirs. Jacques Derrida applied his post-structuralist thinking to the park, advocating 'deconstruction'. This theory was put into practice by architect Peter Eisenman and – it being 1987 at the time – it was no wonder then that a Pomo park was the end result. The striking oversized red waypoint sculptures and rigid walking lines are formal and perhaps profound; certainly there is no park anywhere like this one and its individuality sticks in the mind. Drunk patrons wearing bizarre clothes at such festivals as Pitchfork Paris, taking place at the Grand Halle de la Villette, having stumbled out of a gig by Warpaint or Cigarettes After Sex, would probably agree that this surreal site is the perfect one for such shenanigans.

ENGLISH GARDENS

Munich, Germany

Perambulations through Munich inevitably bring one to the English Gardens, bigger than Central Park and with an epic Capability Brown-esque quality to its meadows and oaks that make the urban cowboy think Kubrick could have shot *Barry Lyndon* here. The quirk of this park is the surfers who ride the waves of the Isar tributaries. There are also sedimentary islands in the stream where visitors take off their shoes to paddle out to and picnic on. Don't be surprised to witness a lot of floppy flesh braising slowly on summer afternoons – this is Deutschland, of course, where pale bratwursts are whipped out at the drop of a Tyrolean hat. As with the Tiergarten in Berlin, slip-slop-slap is combined with swinging and swaying extremities and a realization that the human body has scarcely a surface on it that will refuse to sprout hair.

The Hidden History of Parks

Travis Elborough
author of *A Walk in the Park*

What did you find most interesting about researching the history of parks?

One of the most interesting things was realizing (or discovering, really) that parks are just so full of fascinating contradictions. As public areas, they are sometimes the only places urban residents can go to be private. The lonely can be among company, and even discover companionship, and those seeking solitude can equally find some space to be by themselves. Full of life, there are often also war memorials, like the one to the fallen of Hackney Wick in Victoria Park. The more recent trend for putting name plaques on park benches has added to the idea that they are secular gardens of remembrance.

And what was most surprising?

In many respects the most surprising thing is how comparatively recent they are. While, effectively, we can trace something close to a park-like landscape back to ancient Mesopotamia, and there were earlier iterations of common land and commercial pleasure grounds, and obviously landed country estates, but the public park in Britain as an open-to-all entity is less than 200 years old. As an idea, they emerged – like sewers, democratic government, trade unions and public libraries – in the 19th century and in response to industrialization and rapid urbanization. And initially, they came with certain patrician values baked in about improving the lot of the poor, physically, environmentally, spiritually and morally – and we still discern some of those pedagogical tendencies in modern parks with their nature trails, labelled trees and outdoor gyms. But hence, in their infancy, all that 'Keep Off the Grass' stuff and the authorities were in many instances seriously worried about how people would use the parks. Coming off that, another slight

The Swiss Bridge at Birkenhead Park, Merseyside, UK.

surprise was the sheer amount of fencing in Victorian parks and all the rules and limitations, especially on which games could and couldn't be played in them (quoits and archery, yes; football, frequently, until the 1890s, no.)

Which parks caught your attention in your research?

There were loads but Birkenhead is quite special. It was laid out by Joseph Paxton in his first solo foray into public park making. The American landscape architect Frederick Law Olmsted, who visited it on tour of Britain in 1850, wrote enthusiastically about it subsequently in his book *Walks and Talks of an American Farmer in England* and in the US press. Olmsted later always cited it as a formative influence on his thinking when he eventually came, with Calvert Vaux, to draw up his proposal for Central Park in New York. There's also a slight irony now that Central Park has its Strawberry Fields memorial garden to John Lennon, while when The Beatles were starting out one of the toughest places they found to play, supposedly, was Birkenhead, as they were frequently menaced by the local teddy boys. I also have a real soft spot for Hull's East Park, and particular its rock feature known as the Khyber Pass, partially fashioned in Pulhamite

– the fake rock widely used to create Alpine-style rockeries and mini-me Reichenbach-type water features in the 1870s and beyond. The East Park was opened to celebrate Queen Victoria's Golden Jubilee. Both Victoria's Golden and Diamond Jubilees were something of a spur to public park building in Britain and local councils vied against one another to erect civic monuments to the monarch. (Another reason was to provide work during a prolonged economic slump.) But I've been thinking about this recently and, while I am a republican, it's a shame that HM Queen Elizabeth's platinum year of 2022 wasn't (as far as I know) marked with the creation of a few more green spaces given the climate emergency.

And which park do you like personally to spend time in?

During the pandemic I scarcely went out of Stoke Newington, to be honest. But even if they weren't some of the nearest to me, I'd still probably cite Clissold Park and Victoria Park as among my favourite places to while away an hour or two in. Victoria's model boating lake, during the summer months when the club holds its contests, always makes me smile. Also I love the view of the railway lane and the River Lea from the top of Springfield Park a little further up the road from me in Hackney. I must also mention Southwark Park, which I was honoured to be asked to serve as a patron.

Do you think parks say something about the way we make cities – how you can see them evolve over time?

A great strength of parks is that even the most traditional have proved surprisingly adept at responding to the changing shape of society. Community festivals, outdoor gyms, pop concerts and Tai Chi classes have slotted in beside cricket pitches in the shadows of High Victorian drinking fountains and rock gardens. Eid celebrations in the likes of Goodmayes Park and Southall Park have joined tennis and open-air cinema screenings as eagerly anticipated fixtures of English summers. And that's rather wonderful. But yes, public parks are real barometers of the state of urban life. They were born in response to the after-effects of the Industrial Revolution and lots of the things we associate with older parks, from ornamental 'carpet-bedded' flower beds and lush lawns to bandstands, were themselves products of industrial manufacturing – the heated iron and glass houses and fertilizers needed to cultivate all that greenery and flora, etc. Whereas today rewilding parts of parks and less intensive styles of planting makes much more environmental sense. There's been a move in more recent decades (and pioneered in Scandinavia and elsewhere in Europe) towards linear parks, parks that are less obviously separated from the rest of any given cityscape. Sheffield has done some interesting things in this vein, greening up areas of post-industrial wastelands in the city centre. Obviously there are things like the High Line in New York and the Green Link (Parkland Walk) between Finsbury Park and Highgate in London along another old railway line. Perhaps the direction of travel should be to make all cities more like living in a big park, more London overgrown than underground, and banish some of the distinctions. As I've written elsewhere, are all those gates and fences to protect the park? Or vice versa, to stop the greenery from infecting the city?

What do you think is the kind of quintessential feature about the park, the real reason it's a special place?

The lack of any real financial compulsion to do, or perhaps more importantly to buy, anything very much, continues to be one of their best features. That, almost above all else, is what we must strive to preserve.

AUGARTEN

Vienna, Austria

The formal French-style gardens at the Augarten are unusual examples of rigid design and specific planting that evoke Les Tuileries in Paris, or, even nearer to here, the gardens at Schloss Belvedere. Dating back to the 1700s, the gardens were established for an aristocratic sort to enjoy – Mozart himself conducted concerts here. When the park was opened as a public amenity for the city suddenly anyone could come and enjoy the beauty of the flowers and plants and the Palais Augarten – which is today used by the Vienna Boys' Choir. I was struck by something else the first time I was here, though – the two monstrous concrete Flakturms (flak towers) produced by Organisation Todt, which were installed right at the end of the Second World War in anticipation of a cataclysmic Allied air raid along the lines of Hamburg, Cologne and Dresden. Thankfully for the historic fabric of Vienna, this never came – the Allies deemed Austria to be an occupied nation and (mostly) spared the city. The Flakturms are almost impossible to blow up and remain as an eyesore, albeit a potent one.

TURIA
RIVERBED

Valencia, Spain

How strange that we meddle in nature and expect it not to bite us on the backside. If we insist on building, on concreting, on messing – then what do we expect? That's not to say we should not build. We have to do something, we can't live in reed huts without electricity. But with watercourses one wonders how far is too far: Valencia diverted its river after a torrid flood in 1957 and ended up with a redundant riverbed in the city centre. Can you believe they originally wanted to put a highway on here? That was the equivalent of suggesting someone bring a famished lion to a children's party. General Franco's green credentials weren't noted. After a great many years a park system came instead in the 1980s, led by architects. Ricardo Bofill's formal 1986 gardens and Santiago Calatrava's ridiculously overblown City of Arts and Sciences from 1998 are obviously where eager beavers first head (the latter is so problematic locals protest against it on a semi-regular basis). But there are other sections too that function more like conventional city parks.

TIERGARTEN

Berlin, Germany

Berlin's sprawling Tiergarten says, I think, so much about the urban character of the Hauptstadt. Here are all the signifiers for the city. Berlin seems to have so much space, in fact space seems to be the city's defining characteristic. So many cities feel claustrophobic, but Berlin's history of destruction and division has given it so many random and redundant spaces, whether vacant lots or garden communities or green spaces built on wartime rubble like Teufelsberg or Volkspark Friedrichshain. At the Tiergarten this sense of space is evident too in the sprawling tracts of woodland and lawn. Two more typically Berlin tropes are electronic music and people existing outside the mainstream, both of which were celebrated in huge Love Parades reaching a crescendo at the end of the 1990s, when a million people would fill the Strasse des 17 Juni. Berlin's post-war rebuilding saw modernist architects flock to the city and in the Tiergarten there is the wonderful Hansaviertel. Built in 1957 for the Interbau exhibition, there are modernist masterworks of housing by the likes of Walter Gropius, Arne Jacobsen, Werner Düttmann, Alvar Aalto and Oscar Niemeyer, set – as the modernists wanted it – around the luxuriant parkland that was to define the future city. A section of my novel *The Wall in the Head* takes place here in the Hansaviertel among these landscapes that I find so fascinating. Other quintessentially Berlin things you find in the Tiergarten: the triumphal architecture of the Prussian empire (the Sigessäule statue and the Brandenburg Gate), biergartens, nudist sunbathing spots with their own showers.

HOFGARTEN

Düsseldorf, Germany

Claiming to be Germany's oldest public park
and dating from 1769, the Hofgarten is indeed
a storied set of landscapes set between
Düsseldorf's shopping district and the curving,
flood-prone Rhine. The park (along with the art
scene, exuberant tram network, brilliant airport
and cornucopia of interesting architecture)
makes this city immensely liveable. It's no
wonder those who dwell on the Rhine treasure
the experience so much. A stroll through
the Hofgarten is memorable for its formal
planting, fountains and ponds populated with
young swans who swim around then come up
to the beach and swagger about. Designer
Maximilian Weyhe would surely be intrigued to
see how the park is used by city residents and
visitors today, with ice creams eaten and bikes
ridden on paths below evergreen trees. Weyhe
even used to live in his masterwork in a house
he designed himself.

GRAND PARK

Tirana, Albania

I had an idea to strip down and swim in the big artificial lake that batsh*t dictator Enver Hoxha ordered built here. I have one word of advice: don't. Sadly the water is poisonous and as in need of a clean-up as a fridge in a student house. But Tirana is a city that I love despite its scruffiness, and the rest of this park is in good shape, much of it having been recently restored. It dates back to the 1950s and there are various whimsical pieces of architecture like a super-cute theatre for children's shows and a circular modernist pergola atop the hill. Several cafés bring people in to read the paper and chat and the paths are perfect for runners. You can spy the American School, a Communist-era café where the lake water comes right up into the gardens, and yes, there's a road train for the lazy or infirm. It feels wild and is great for a leg stretch, but please, guys, get the litter cleared up. Faleminderit.

BLATTERWIESE

Zürich, Switzerland

The first time I came here I was rather surprised to see the Pavillon Le Corbusier in a shocking state of repair – peering inside it seemed as if someone had had a party and fled before the parents arrived. This was a few years ago and now the pavilion has been restored to its 1967 glory. It's a strange beast though, an art museum that looks more like a petrol station, and with its flashes of primary colours was Corb's final flourish before he swam out to sea at Roquebrune-Cap-Martin one last time – as ways to die go, a very solid choice. The park it sits in skirts Lake Zürich and has an interesting history as the site of the Swiss National Exhibition in 1939 and the G59 Garden Exhibition in 1959. There's a Chinese pagoda and garden with an exotic collection of plums, bamboo, pine and willow, and a water palace surrounded by a lake.

ŁAZIENKI PARK

Warsaw, Poland

Warsaw is something of a revelation – a very cool, increasingly Westernized capital that seems to be motoring ahead, and despite the best efforts of a crackpot right-leaning central government the city and its altogether more liberal council and citizens seem to enjoy life, one example of which is strolling at the weekend in this beautiful royal park. I was struck by how clean and well kept it all seemed, a result of huge investment since the fall of Communism. The manicured formal gardens sitting in front of baroque palaces, with peacocks parading around, give a sense of serenity and posh charm. One of my favourite parts of the park is the classical amphitheatre from 1793, set in a lake and linked to land via a causeway. It just looks like the perfect place to perform a play and must surely have been the hottest ticket in town among the well-heeled and powerful invited to come and watch back in its heyday. The whole park feels quite French-influenced, like a Versailles in the east, but today is a place where anyone from Warsaw can come for an afternoon out with the kids.

Sustainability

Harriet Thorpe
Architecture writer and journalist

What kind of sustainable architecture can you see in parks?

Architecture has always been a joyful part of a park's infrastructure – whether it's a sports pavilion, a coffee kiosk or a public toilet. Those little, super-functional buildings help embed parks into our daily urban life. Yet today, their role is increasingly critical. Climate change and population growth are putting increased pressure on parks, and they need to be protected and nourished like never before. Architecture can help – not only by being zero-carbon, low-energy and low-maintenance, but by actively encouraging biodiversity. That could mean with a green roof, a water-harvesting system connected to the landscape, nesting boxes, or space for education about wildlife.

What sustainability innovations in park design can you see?

When thoughtfully designed, city parks can reduce pollution, prevent flooding and strengthen ecosystems. The 'sponge city' concept (increasingly being discussed by cities across the world) shows how water can be cleverly absorbed by parks through systems of terracing, ponding and dyking, dependent on climate and inspired by indigenous thinking. The concept has a multitude of benefits – including naturally cleaning water and preventing concrete-heavy industrial alternatives. In Sydney Park 44 hectares of land have been designed as bio-retention wetlands with ponds and ebbing channels, which capture and clean water to supply 10 per cent of the city's water demand, all while contributing to natural habitats and providing space for leisure. Meanwhile, in tropical Taiwan, a series of microclimates have been designed into Taichung's 67-hectare Central Park, a former airport site. Using water basins and planting, the park's design helps make the city cooler, drier and less polluted. Cool areas feature densely planted forest and hairy-leaved trees reduce air pollution near the children's playgrounds – after all, it's a park for people too. There are solar-powered pavilions and interactive sensors measuring heat, humidity and pollution.

Are parks too cultivated? Should we let the land be more wild?

Yes! Most parks prioritize humans, but we need to adjust that balance to prioritize plants and wildlife. We should be getting comfortable with more wildness in parks, and actively 'rewilding' them. Less cultivation has lots of benefits to the environment – letting native plants and animals flourish of their own accord can help rebuild the ecosystems that many cities are losing; and denser planting absorbs more carbon to keep the air cleaner, proved by the Miyawaki method, which is encouraging an urban mini-forest movement. Campaigns such as 'No Mow May' in the UK or 'National Pollinator Week'

in the US are spreading popular awareness about rewilding, along with the UN's Decade on Ecosystem Restoration launched in 2021.

Could the sustainability agenda change the definition of a park as we know it today?

Definitely, and in many ways – parks are becoming multi-tasking pieces of green infrastructure that draw on the natural functions of the Earth to solve many of the problems that we have created through urbanization. Water will play more of a key role, and they might be much wilder, denser and filled with more types of animals. Yet also, hopefully in the not too distant future, parks will permeate and reclaim cities until they are blended green, making them healthier places to live. It's happening already – Barcelona is planting parks in former streets to create pedestrian-friendly routes through the city for more shade and less pollution, while in a Madrid suburb, citizens are taking their right to green space into their own hands with a guerrilla mini-forest of 1,500 trees planted on derelict, unused land, the Bosque Urbano. Sustainability is about our continued healthy survival on this planet, and parks have a huge part to play in this future.

HEYSEL

Brussels, Belgium

Laeken Park sits to the east of the Heysel
Plateau, offering conventional greenery
and water features and plenty of places
to picnic. But at Heysel's centre sits a
magnificent memory of why this place was
so important – the Atomium. Its huge balls
were the focal point for the 1958 Expo – one
of the most important events of modern
architecture, which laid out in detail what
the rapidly approaching 1960s were going
to look like as the world totally transformed
into a global system with cars, computers,
airports, skyscrapers and mass housing all
making their swaggering mark on society.
To walk these tree-lined avenues during that
year must have been delicious; it's a scene
Jonathan Coe paints with panache in his
bravura novel *Expo 58*. And even before that
point Heysel was a centre for design: the clean
lines of the buildings from the 1935 World's
Fair scintillate, the city's Design Museum is
based here; and there's of course a football
stadium synonymous with the tragedy of the
1985 European Cup Final. Oh, and a miniature
version of all the countries of Europe. No
Smurfs, though. If you are hungry go to the
Quick branch here for one of their bonkers
burgers served between two bits of toast, the
esteemed Quick N Toast.

ZARYADYE PARK

Moscow, Russia

Zaryadeye Park strikes you at first as over-engineered, the park equivalent of using a hammer (or perhaps a sickle) to crack a nut. There are a lot of buildings for a start. But there was a whole lot more building before: the infamous Rossiya stood here from the 1960s to the 2000s, the foreigners' hotel where the KGB stalked the corridors and listened in on every conversation. When that was pulled down an opportunity presented itself for a new public space right next to Red Square and the river – the 'floating bridge' poised above the water is, we could probably say, the 'icon' of this park, but there are also theatres, concert halls and museums woven into the fabric of Diller Scofidio + Renfro's 2017 design. But there seems not to be much in the way of greenery as you try to negotiate the pathways on the sloping site. Still, it was an emblem of how Moscow tried to modernize, to Westernize, to tidy and green itself. Let's hope Russia's wars end soon so the visitors can return.

AMERICAS

FREEWAY PARK

Seattle, USA

The number one question I find people ask when you write books like this is: 'Which is your favourite ...' and I think I already have a favourite park. I discovered it a few years ago on a meander through Seattle and it blew my mind. It was like stumbling on Aztec ruins – the huge concrete blocks arrayed around barely still functioning water features under a tree canopy. It all provided a weird mix of prehistoric, dystopian future and retro-chic. The park sits atop a freeway and provides space for citizens to lunch and a pedestrian route between two parts of the city cheese-wired in two by Interstate 5. It's surreal and a lot for your brain to process in one go. The sublime nature of the park made me go home and read everything I could about designer Lawrence Halprin. I went to see his other landscaping projects – the Keller Fountain Park in Portland, Oregon, the landscaping of the BART stations in San Francisco and Gateway Park in Rosslyn, Virginia. But Freeway Park is his masterwork and a genuinely bizarre addition to downtown Seattle – it's also being restored in 2023 with millions of dollars of funding.

IBIRAPUERA PARK

São Paulo, Brazil

With landscape design by Roberto Burle Marx and a brace of buildings by legendary left-wing ladies' man Oscar Niemeyer, Ibirapuera Park was conceived around the same time the pair were also working on the superscale plans for Brasilia (as Robert Hughes grumpily proclaimed: 'a ceremonial slum'). Ibirapuera Park is São Paulo's green lung and opened for the city's 400th anniversary celebrations in 1954, giving one of the world's largest metropolises some much-needed breathing space. Among the lawns and tropical trees is a feast of modern architecture and culture – the Modern Art Museum of São Paulo, the Museum of Contemporary Art, the Museum Afro-Brazil, the Planetarium, the Biennial Pavilion, the Japanese Pavilion and a later work by Niemeyer – the Ibirapuera Auditorium (2002–05) – which looks like a gigantic wedge of Wensleydale with a red tongue poking provocatively out of the front, ready to lick a passing giant. There's a huge ceremonial lake and the main road through the park is named after legendary Brazilian F1 ace Ayrton Senna.

MILLENNIUM PARK AND GRANT PARK

Chicago, USA

Plenty of parks feature public art and sculpture, and indeed many parks exist explicitly to display sculpture, such as the Yorkshire Sculpture Park in the UK and Storm King in the USA. But perhaps Millennium Park has got the most instantly noticeable public art icon in the shape of Anish Kapoor's *Cloud Gate*, aka The Bean. *Cloud Gate* has become a sight-bite, a shorthand now for the city itself. Millennium Park dates from 2004 when the rail lines running through this prime slice of Downtown Chicago were covered over. It's a prissy, formal, corporate affair but one which proves very popular, with many visitors keen on eyeing Frank Gehry's bonkers Pritzker Pavilion too. A Gehry bridge (BP Oil have the naming rights to it) snakes over Columbus Drive into the larger and older Grant Park proper. Grant Park dates from the 1840s and its mix of lawns, planting and beaux-arts civic buildings have witnessed many moments in American history: Lincoln's funeral procession in 1865, the 1968 clashes at the Democratic National Convention, Obama's victory speech in 2008. The Lollapalooza rock festival gets the crowds going here too.

CENTRAL PARK

New York, USA

While there were parks *avant la lettre*, Central Park really set a new standard in how large and prestigious (and, well, central) they could be. The act of sacrificing such a swathe of potentially priceless real estate a future generation of terrible Trumps could never mercilessly milk seemed wholly un-American; the destruction of the Black-settled Seneca Village to build the park was more predictable. An enormous rectangle of green space was created in the heart of Manhattan that would one day make the perfect backdrop for *Home Alone 2*. The Little Leaguers practising their swings always seem so cute, so does the skating rink and the various lakes teeming with fowl. The bizarre sight of horse-and-carriage rides taking bemused tourists trotting round the southern park is surely destined for the history books one of these days. With 42 million visits recorded in 2020, Central Park is one of the world's most popular urban parks. Many visitors just stroll but runners come to circumnavigate the Jacqueline Kennedy Onassis Reservoir and from June to September swimmers can take a dip at the Lasker Pool. Overlooking the park are plenty of interesting buildings, the Guggenheim Museum on Fifth Avenue being one of the best.

STANLEY PARK

Vancouver, Canada

As with so much about the city of Vancouver, Stanley Park is instantly likeable. Its wilderness feel is not hugely sculpted by the hand of man – there are forests that stretch to the end of the downtown peninsula, and if you keep your eyes open you can spot coyotes, skunks and raccoons among the firs, hemlocks and spruces. The rainy climate makes everything almost self-consciously green. Swimmers congregate down at Second Beach and kids will love the miniature railway that traverses the park. The seawall is the place for walking and running and Beaver Lake adds another watery flavour. There's also a popular pitch-and-putt course. Obviously, land is a contentious issue in a country where Europeans came and claimed it for themselves. An array of First Nations totems elucidates the people who were custodians of this land first and gateways carved in a traditional Salish style showcase vernacular architecture and remind visitors that the history of the area stretches back much further than to the 1888 official opening of the park.

GRIFFITH PARK

Los Angeles, USA

Numerous movies have been shot in Griffith Park but I rather like the way the park gets to play itself in a very obvious and celebratory way in *La La Land*, when Emma Stone and Ryan Gosling go into the Griffith Observatory and then dance and flirt and look for their parked cars around the Cathy's Corner section. In a movie that trumpets LA against the doubters it's apt that the park plays a big part, because for Angelinos this is a place that you will eventually get to, and for some it's a place that they come to as often as possible. The relative serenity you can find, the views over the horribly sprawling metropolis and the scent of pine in the Berlin Forest above the Observatory all whisk you away (if you can find a parking spot). There's something about being in the hills too – the Hollywood wannabes that jog the paths, wanting to spy the sign, to keep themselves firm for the next audition, dreaming of success and a house up here as a mark of success ... well, that's me too, in a way. One day, LA. This is the city of dreams. I've stood by the Observatory wondering about a future where LA will figure, and my stupid name will be up in lights when we sell the film rights to this very book and make the greatest movie about parks anyone has ever put to celluloid. Are Emma Stone's people able to confirm if she can be attached to the project?

ROSE KENNEDY GREENWAY

Boston, USA

Walking the 'Greenway' along Boston's waterfront is like a small trick is being played on you. You know something isn't quite right – but what is it? What's missing? Ah yes, it's the freeway. Interstate 93 is beneath our feet as we walk the slim, linear park, buried as part of the Big Dig project that aimed to reunite Boston and the water by removing the grossly overengineered elevated highway structure along which cars and trucks thundered, returning the space to some kind of calm and to the realm of pedestrians. A similar highway-removal trick has been played in other forward-looking cities like Seattle and San Francisco, and you wonder whether all of these elevated highways will eventually end up in the ground, for the sake of the environment and perhaps for the value of the land that they sit on too. Here on the Greenway you can find reminders of the road in the sense of emptiness and the elongated shape of the extended park and in the ventilation towers. Various parks within a park, with their own character, sit on the Greenway – the Carolyn Lynch Garden filled with colourful, seasonal blooms, the Armenian Heritage Park, the Chinese-themed Auntie Kay and Uncle Frank Chin Park, Dewey Square Park with its rain garden and mini-orchard, and the North End Parks with their water features. There's a carousel, plenty of public art and food trucks galore to sate the appetites of lunching Bostonians.

MOUNT ROYAL PARK

Montreal, Canada

Sweeping views over Montreal are your reward for yomping up to the mini-summit of Mount Royal Park. If you've had too many Timbits at breakfast you can drive your car up the road to the car park. The typically French cemetery offers macabre gravestones and creepy swaying trees aplenty, plus foxes, while the park proper is the 1876 work of Frederick Law Olmsted, who also designed, of course, Central Park and Prospect Park in New York City as well as parks in Buffalo, Milwaukee and Louisville. In winter you can come here to sledge and even ski, and that lookout grants you great views of Montreal's amazing hipster neighbourhoods and cornucopia of modern architecture left over from the fecund period between Expo 67 and the 1976 Olympics – before Montreal fell on hard times and Toronto took over as Canada's primary metropolis. Lovers: it is also famed as a proposal spot.

The High Line Effect

If Lyle Lanley was the shyster selling stuff to the citizens of Springfield today it wouldn't be a monorail he'd be flogging - it would be a park in the sky. That classic *Simpsons* episode hit the nail on the head in taking down a generation of American cities (Detroit, Miami; Honolulu is late to the party) who fell for the dubious (though let the record show I love them and ride on any I can find) appeal of a robotic train running above the rooftops. That era seems to be waning slightly - now it's parks we crane our necks to look up at.

The High Line wasn't there first. There were parks on disused elevated railway lines *avant la lettre*: if Paris's 1993 Coulée Verte René-Dumont - aka La Promenade Plantée - was the Nokia, and London's 1984 Parkland Walk from Finsbury Park to Alexandra Palace was the Motorola, the High Line was the Apple iPhone.

The first High Line stage opened in 2009 and immediately ignited the popular imagination. No holiday or business trip to New York in the 2010s was thinkable without a walk along its length through the Meatpacking District and Chelsea. It's since been expanded up to Hudson Yards, a place where an architectural blitzkrieg has scorched the earth, where real-estate money stopped caring about covering its tracks and just said: 'To hell with it all.' This is where Kendall Roy stares out from the balcony

Above: La Promenade Plantée, Paris, France. Pages 124–125: The High Line, New York, USA.

Folkestone Harbour Arm, UK.

of his crushingly lonely bachelor pad in *Succession* as his life and mind collapse in the way of 40-something men who are too drunk on dosh and power; where he hosts the most grotesquely debased and hollow rich-boy birthday party, telling the long-suffering PR without irony: 'My thing from the very first meeting was that it shouldn't feel like an asshole's birthday party', Jeremy Strong playing him like a sleep-walking Patrick Bateman crossed with a doe-eyed basset hound caught taking a dump.

Is the High Line guilty by association? Is this just window-dressing – gentrification by stealth? Or can we trust it? Certainly we sometimes like it, we go there and it feels calming among the hustle to watch the pampas sway, to feel it tickle the neck, to sit on the benches and look at the old rail lines and sleepers, to imagine the railcars clattering overhead when the city was so very different, to even imagine the trains running on the street before the elevated line was built (lots of people got killed, unsurprisingly). Hudson Yards put a lid over the Long Island Rail Road lines and erected depressing skyscrapers and an icon that the depressed could jump from (The Vessel) and which has had to be periodically closed due to the suicides. The High Line's planting programme creates serenity and a kind of classiness that makes you feel you're in a walk 'n' talk from a TV show when you're strolling with friends and a coffee. The glamour is enhanced by the celebrities who funded or supported the whole project – the likes of Marion Cotillard, Kevin Bacon, Ed Norton, Glenn Close. But you look at the exorbitant new 'industrial' apartments and the Elephant's Foot Building, a brutalist sort-of-icon reclad comically in glass yet the same shape, and ponder the smoke and mirrors.

A new sculpture over the road from that building, near the top of the High Line, makes you wonder what's going on – is all in the skypark world as cosy as it seems? Sam Durant's fibreglass copy of a Predator drone – the kind that silently and mercilessly creep through the skies of the Middle East and the Horn of Africa, destroying humans with an icy precision, the trigger pulled from far away – is certainly some kind of provocation. I wonder who is being provoked?

What's beyond a doubt is how the 'success' of the High Line has spread around the USA and around the world. Cities are queueing up for their own piece of the pie. Atlanta has its Beltline, Rotterdam its Hofbogen. Folkestone in south-east England has started a kind of High Line on its old Harbour Branch Line. The Bloomingdale Line in Chicago became the 606 in 2015, Philadelphia has the Rail Park. In London the Camden Highline is to be built next to the North London Line. The Goods Line very obviously takes its cues from the High Line as it stretches through Ultimo in Sydney and down towards the harbour, its nooks now home to the homeless. The Riverline will be coming to Buffalo in 2023.

What's maybe perplexing about this trend is that rail is actually making a comeback as a green transport alternative. Should we be keeping the tracks themselves open? The city is all about balancing – and trying to find the balance between space for rapid transit and for pedestrians and cyclists is a hot topic. Indeed, one of the points of the High Line and its imitators is that walking the city needs to be encouraged. For Europeans who are by nature *flâneurs* and *flâneuses* this is a no-brainer. In anywhere in the USA that is not New York City, though, walking understandably needs a push. We come full circle to the monorail, because the latest iteration of this kind of park is found right underneath Miami's Downtown Metromover structure. The Underline is a new park project that brings life beneath those pesky monorail supports. Even lower is New York's Low Line, the next frontier for parks – an underground park proposed in a redundant tram terminal.

The Underline, Miami, USA.

ASIA AND AFRICA

YOYOGI PARK & MEIJI JINGU SHRINE PARK

Tokyo, Japan

Once again we find the best brutalist icons incongruously located inside parks in what is becoming an interesting trend. Weird? Not really – for all their otherworldliness and camp grandeur, the buildings these modernist architects designed were often all about landscape too – they wanted parkland around their chefs-d'oeuvre, and so Kenzo Tange's bravura gymnastic hall for the Tokyo 1964 Olympics stands proud today in Yoyogi Park. The springtime cherry blossoms draw tourists here from far and wide, so too do the intriguing subcultures of young Tokyo residents who gather to find an escape route from a strict society. I remember watching these youngsters do their thing as Elvis or some kind of computer-game character on a Michael Palin travelogue TV show in the 1990s, long before I'd even been to Japan. Seeing it in real life was as gloriously surreal as you'd imagine, and here we have parks being used for what they're best at – just letting you be, giving you space, allowing you to do things in groups, in a free public realm, without the need to buy anything and conform to anything. Those conventions come back with a bang when you cross into the Meiji Jingu Shrine Park though – the beautiful parkland shrine buildings are dotted with polite people washing and praying: for their daughter to find a husband, for their son to find a job, for their cancer to clear.

135

RIZAL PARK

Manila, Philippines

Waxing and waning of empire and power itself seems writ large in Rizal Park – which is now named for the hero-martyr Dr Rizal, who wrote novels and was killed by the Spanish here; a memorial commemorates the spot where he got a bullet for his troubles. Called Luneta Park when the Spanish dignitaries walked here after leaving the walled-in safety of their stronghold at Intramuros, a little to the north, the park has always been at the centre of things in Manila. In the sticky air I watched the huge Philippine flag that flies on the corner of Roxas Boulevard almost fluttering, steadfastly saying its piece about a new Philippine Republic that has had plenty of hard times, tears and troubles but is at least notionally free now. Yet the Americans who dominated after the Spaniards have their embassy right across the street. Daniel Burnham, whose plans for San Francisco I explored in my previous book *Unbuilt*, formulated a plan to build beaux-arts government buildings all around the park at one stage. Political rallies were held here. I'd walked here along the coastal promenade from the Cultural Center of the Philippines, a brutalist beast inaugurated by notorious shoe bulk-buyer Imelda Marcos as her pet project, and remembered the Marcoses held rallies here too at the height of their cult-like power, before the downfall came hard. And Popes Francis and John Paul II have both brought millions of the devout to pray in this park for some of the largest gatherings ever recorded.

LUMPHINI PARK

Bangkok, Thailand

Memories of Bangkok – notices in the hotel room forbidding durian fruit and, weirdly perhaps, ads all over town for the first season of *Sex Education* (I'm not complaining, it's one of my favourite ever Netflix shows). And the oppressive urbanity of it all. The Skytrain cuts through the traffic and drops you outside Lumphini Park, which provides a degree of respite from the tourists and the traffic, but not from the noxious air. The artificial lake here hints at what the stopover tourists are really after – the sea and beaches down at the coast. The trees barely sway in the stultifying air, but here is a place where you can at least catch your breath, briefly. Joggers, yoga practitioners, walkers find solace. Bizarre birds flutter around, making you ponder their strange species, and various events are staged – some kind of tourism show was taking place when I was here. Every kind of person in a suit or dress was trying to get me to come and take a leaflet about something or other.

FORT CANNING PARK

Singapore

The quintessential Singapore park, Fort Canning teems with interesting sights that have witnessed their fair share of history. The Battlebox, where the British realized it was game over against the Japanese in 1942, is under the park's soil and the governor used to live in a house in the park. A replica of Government House – which was actually first the residence of Stamford Raffles, one of the founders of modern Singapore – sits overlooking the city (Fort Canning Park is on a hill). Raffles was a keen botanist and experimented in gardening, and the British colonial authorities continued those experiments. You can see the preserved experimental gardens, which were planted with nutmeg, cloves, sugarcane and tea plants. There are also plenty of exotic fruit trees around the park, and a lake too.

PEACE MEMORIAL PARK

Hiroshima, Japan

Cemeteries are the most obvious examples of parks dedicated to death, but many memorial and peace parks dot the world too. Hiroshima's brings together a collection of formal landscapes and tranquil gardens to memorialize that which was the opposite of both of those things: horror and slaughter on a previously unimaginable scale. But the language is telling: this is a Peace Park where the catastrophe of the atomic explosion of 1945 is seen as a warning to future generations, that war and weapons of mass destruction must be avoided. Have we learned those lessons? Kenzo Tange's park contains modernist museums and sculptures surrounded by lawns and trees. A mound at the centre contains the ashes of tens of thousands, peace bells toll to remind us; the miraculously surviving A-Bomb Dome building stands as a kind of monument to a human spirit that could not be crushed.

XUHUI RUNWAY PARK

Shanghai, China

An eco-conscious park that makes use of the 'sponge city' principle with water gardens and runoff areas to encourage rainwater to permeate and storms to be mitigated, Xuhui Runway Park was designed by Sasaki Architects and opened in 2020. The park takes its cues from the former Longhua Airport and military base. Just up the road, near to another park – the Shanghai Botanical Garden – the young J. G. Ballard was imprisoned with his family in Longhua internment camp, a story told with bravado in *Empire of the Sun* and an experience that was to shape one of our greatest 20th-century writers. Today those memories seem a million miles away in ambivalent, tech-savvy modern China. The children's play area has cute runway-esque designs and the park as a whole is designed to emphasize the length and shape of the former runways, with long paths and bamboo boardwalks, and wetland plants and irises adding the natural touches.

Festivals

Andre D. L. McLeod
Travel and lifestyle journalist,
party organiser

What are your first memories of being at a festival in a park?

One of the first proper memories of being at a major event in a park would be the Lambeth Country Show when I was 12 years old. This is an annual festival/carnival held in Brockwell Park. I used to volunteer at Vauxhall City Farm when I was a kid, cleaning up all the poo, giving rides on Jacko the donkey and learning how to ride horses. Every summer, they took a selection of animals down to the park for the weekend to showcase the farm. I used to muck in, speak to punters about the animals and generally sneak off and take in the festivities. One year my dad dropped me off as usual and gave me some money for the day. This would normally be like a tenner or 20 quid at most, but today was a special day. Today was my 12th birthday, on the cusp of teenagerhood. In celebration of this momentous occasion, my old man gave me a whole £50 this time!

What a day to be alive. Freshly minted, I quickly did all my tasks in the tent for the farm and set off into the Country Show with a spring in my step. Funfair rides, bumper cars, burgers, hot dogs and all the fizzy drinks were splurged on over the day. I felt like a millionaire, and this was my playground. Forget Monaco. When my Dad came to pick me up, he told me he had given me that fifty by mistake but left me to it as was my birthday. Great day all round!

Which parks are best for festivals?

Victoria Park, Clapham Common and Brockwell Park come to mind.

Tell us about some festivals you remember in parks.

Two of the first festivals I remember attending would be SW4 in Clapham Common and Lovebox in Victoria Park. Both were really fun and were not only my first ones but also my first as press, so I had access not afforded to regular folk: backstage, VIP bar and clean toilets. Clapham Common is one of the closest major parks to where I lived, so the location and ease of access were amazing. Just a quick bus and a hop and a skip and I was there. I can't remember who played that year, tbh, but what I do remember was that Nandos had a tent in the backstage area, and I walked away with a load of grub that day! Lovebox is a festival I've attended many times and as it normally falls on my birthday is a great way to celebrate. Have seen so many artists over the years and drunk many drinks in the VIP areas. The dance music stages are always fun, tucked away surrounded by trees like a hidden forest with a giant disco ball bouncing and refracting light from day till night. It feels a bit like the Ewoks partying in the woods after defeating the Empire. Have attended other really fun festivals like Eastern Electrics, Field Day, All Points East and Wireless many times over the years.

Why are parks better than other festival venues?

I think that festivals in parks are better for many reasons. I like a local location. There's something appealing about knowing that after a long day dancing and frolicking in the park, it's nice to have a quick bus or train ride home to your own bed and fridge.

Which parks outside London are great for festivals?

TRNSMT festival (formerly T In The Park) in Glasgow Green is great. The cool thing about it is that its location is so central. You walk to it from the big train stations and buses stop near it. Also, Parklife in Manchester – I think I went to Heaton Park in 2013 but don't remember a lot, as I was with my friend and his uni mates studying in Manchester, but what I do recall was a fun and lively festival again a short bus ride from his flat. Definitely a trend developing.

Which park festivals around the world do you want to go to but haven't?

So many come to mind, and as a travel writer, the list is endless, but the main ones would be Rock in Rio Lisboa in Parque da Bela Vista, Lisbon, We Love Green festival in the Bois de Vincennes, Paris, and Lollapalooza in Olympiapark Berlin. I run my own party brand called We Got This! which specializes in creating house party-style events around London at venues like The Ministry Members club, Rotate Shoreditch and London Bridge Rooftop. I'm looking at possibly doing my own festival in an 18th-century palace located in a small park in Poland. A mini boutique festival with friends, banging tunes and delicious food in an incredible location. That's the plan anyway!

HOUTAN PARK

Shanghai, China

Whether or not parks are good or bad for the environment is a moot point. They preserve land from development and provide space for all kinds of flora and fauna to bloom. Yet they are also inherently unnatural habitats that are carefully managed and maintained at great expense, which sometimes trounce on the 'real' natural world and obviously attract many extra visitors. You can run yourself round in circles thinking about what is best. At Shanghai's Houtan Park a conscious decision was made to try and create something that was ecologically grounded, which in the 'full steam ahead' China of 2010 was perhaps not the priority that was realized it must be a decade down the line, with ever more data about climate change in the bank and our worry levels cranked up. So it's interesting then that Turenscape landscape architects offered this vision as part of the Shanghai Expo: a river park that would clean polluted water – 600,000 litres daily, in fact, using natural means, actively promoting biodiversity (90-plus species of plants and 200-plus animals) and also taking carbon out of the air. The linear park uses reedbeds, bamboo and redwoods, and adds in sunflowers and traditional terraced gardens with seasonal plants, and large industrial-style metal structures that hark back the site's former life as a steelworks, dock and dump.

VICTORIA PEAK GARDEN

Hong Kong, China

The quintessential day out in Hong Kong is taking the Peak Tram up to the summit of Victoria Peak and marvelling at the eye-popping views down to Central, with its proliferation of skyscrapers. The vertical city reveals itself squeezed in between mountains and the sea, and it is one of the most vital and exciting cityscapes in the world, best viewed twice: once from up here and a second time from the Star Ferry travelling over from Kowloon. Up here where the birds swoop, the temperatures are lower and the air clearer. It's no wonder the old British Governor had the bright idea of building a summer residence. That house is gone but the gardens remain as a public park at the top of the mountain, with pergolas and benches, and views to the west and south of the island on clear days too. There are formal shrubberies and lawns on which you're welcome to picnic.

ZHISHAN GARDENS AND INDIGENOUS PEOPLE'S PARK

Taipei, Taiwan

After a morning's browsing of the bounty of imperial times in the National Palace Museum (do not miss the jasper shaped like a piece of pork belly and the jade shaped like cabbage, but equally do not nibble them if you want to avoid an emergency dental appointment), you might be in need of fresh air. The Zhishan Gardens, below the museum, are some of the nicest in Taipei. Naturally the park is perfectly maintained and cared for, pleasant and inviting – just like everything and everyone in this wonderful capital city that will dazzle those who've become jaded with other grossly polluted Asian megalopolises. Calm reigns supreme – a lake with ducks and geese, an orchid pavilion, and intriguing landscaping elements that come together in the 'four principles' of Chinese gardens – the harmony of plants, water, architecture and rocks. A stone dragon spits water and koi dart about under its spray. Directly across the river the Indigenous People's Park shines a light on the Pacific civilization that was on Formosa before the Chinese and Japanese arrived: totems, tiles, cypress trees and ginger plants present an intriguing picture of traditional life on the island.

SEOULLO 7017 SKYPARK

Seoul, South Korea

An advertisement for the benefits of repurposing rather than demolishing (a topic which is even more important now we see the wastefulness of knocking things down and the environmental impact of that methodology), Seoullo 7017 (built as a highway in 1970, turned into a park in 2017) is an intriguing attempt to make something that was not very friendly into a place you want to stay. I must confess to expecting more in the way of greenery when I was there, but I still think it counts as a park – there are the planters, benches, kiosks and corners to explore that you'd expect in a park. As time goes on the plants should grow taller. MVRDV's design is a pretty simple reworking of this old motorway flyover above Seoul Station and it points a way towards how we can rework other 'concrete island' pieces of road infrastructure. What would J. G. Ballard have made of the way that pedestrians have suddenly been welcomed into the previously sacrosanct autoworld? Now you can stroll where the cars once revved, and I think these kinds of parks will become more popular around the world. São Paulo's Minhocão, a similar but longer overpass, will have 1 kilometre of its end chopped off and turned into a park; it is famously pedestrianized at weekends and is wildly popular with skaters and cyclists.

Playtime

As we get older our tastes split in a million directions; there are so many kinds of things we want, and everyone's desires are slightly different. When we're a kid all we want (and all we're gonna get) is the park. No problemo! It's the only place for little people to be anyway. Do you remember the first time you got on a swing, or a seesaw, or a slide? Here we learn about the world of excitement and anticipation, about risk and danger and what we can get away with, about other kids; about sharing and waiting and creating crazy games dreamed up inside our tiny heads.

As an adult you notice that the kids come with divorced dads or stressed mums, parents with coffees, parents fretting to friends about measles or school catchment areas or the collapse of their sex lives ... or, just sometimes, chilled and happy parents enjoying the fun as much as their kids are.

Children have always played because that's how they learn. Psychologists recognize play as the elemental essence of learning. This playtime is of the utmost importance in the development of tiny, squishy minds. But when massive urbanization hit the Western world after the Industrial Revolution we worried if street and yard play was enough, if it was better for kids to be back in the farms and fields where they were less likely to lose a finger under the wheels

Above: Diana Memorial Playground, Kensington Gardens, London, UK.
Pages 166–167: Churchill Gardens, Pimlico, London, UK.

Coram's Fields, Bloomsbury, London, UK.

of a penny-farthing piloted by a fop named Benedict or something.

Proto-playgrounds came in the 1800s, one to Golden Gate Park in San Francisco in the 1880s, more in New York. Whole parks were devoted to kids – like Coram's Fields in London, where adults without a wee one are prohibited to this day. Kids needed somewhere safe, especially true when the streets became the preserve of the car. Modernist architects recognized that parks must accompany the new estates and towns that rose up, and that kids must be catered for. Goldfinger brought concrete slides to Trellick and Balfron Tower. Powell & Moya built steps that looked like the Giant's Causeway up to a flying saucer at Churchill Gardens. These structures were recreated in a celebratory way by Assemble and artist Simon Terrill in 2015 in an exhibition at RIBA called *The Brutalist Playground*. At the exhibition the copies were made of something softer and foamier so that visitors would not end up with a broken leg.

To direct kids away from danger and to official playgrounds and parks, hilariously chilling public information films were shown in schools to a generation of British kids who were triggered whenever they passed farm machinery or power lines or anything else portrayed in the films as being grossly dangerous.

Today's playgrounds may be less concretey but they still often fizz with imagination. Extravagant tree houses, death slides, games, rope bridges, houses. Playgrounds often have a spongy surface in case your kid falls off a ladder, but the idea remains. Some of the coolest modern designs are the giant sandboxes at places like Arnos Park, where you can turn a tap and flood a ravine, and see how nature works. The crucial thing is to get the fat-fingered little tykes off the PS5 and out of the bloody house. Today's parents are terrified to let little Johnny play outside, but play he must – it's an essential part of childhood.

TABLE MOUNTAIN RESERVE

Cape Town, South Africa

Cities can win or lose in the geographic lottery. Cape Town is a winner. Imagine having this beauty in your backyard. Table Mountain and the parkland surrounding the peak are full of brooding beauty. The mountain gives Cape Town one of the most stunning settings of any city. From the top (once the cloud clears), you won't know whether to stare at the dassies cutely scuttling around or at the cityscape of Cape Town unfurling beneath. It's a park but it sure feels wild up here, with a genuine mountain that you can climb on your own or ascend in a cable car. There are so many types of plants and flowers up here that botanists will think it's Christmas – from neon fynbos flowers to Table Mountain watsonias and Cape daisies. In all there are over 2,000 different species of plants. Keep your eyes open for fauna too: porcupine, mongoose and caracal. It's quite the adventure – hard to believe you're only ten minutes from the centre of one of South Africa's biggest cities.

AUSTRALASIA

BARANGAROO RESERVE

Sydney, Australia

Sydney's newest park juts out into the harbour on a scrappy point that used to be a temporary home to commercial sea freighters, and I remember jogging past the boarded-up old docks on my first visits to Australia more than a decade ago. In a country now totally enslaved to real-estate money like zombies in a bank vault, of course this could not be allowed to continue and the huge Barangaroo development comprises offices for thousands and a soaring casino hotel. The construction traffic during this long period has been intense, and the city's new Metro station under the Barangaroo Reserve has added even more engineering complexity. Although the park opened in 2015 it might take a couple more years before calm really returns to this area. In the meantime, the young park waits until the planting takes hold and things grow, but it functioned well as a venue for some artworks as part of the 2019 Sydney Festival. Jacob Nash's sign spelling out 'ALWAYS' was an invitation to think about the nature of time, possession and this very land, which was of course used for a lot of years before the Rum Corps et al arrived in the 1700s to cause chaos. Naturally there are sweeping harbour views and watching the boats bob is as much fun as checking out the 80 local species of plants put into the new park.

ADELAIDE'S PARKS

Adelaide, Australia

Adelaide Festival, 6 March 2019. With salty water in the corners of my eyes I watched my beloved Beach House make music that sounded like the end of time, if not the end of love. On a scrappy square amid Adelaide University buildings, the band's dreamy soundtrack to one Englishman's evening epiphany made the next section of that night even more poignant. I wandered over to the Kaurna Learning Circle and out into Karrawirra Park, surrounded by *son et lumière* installations that paid tribute to the original custodians of this land who were here long before Europeans designated it as a park or indeed anything else. Stories told by speakers, illuminated animals cutting through the night sky. As I walked I realized something, something that will be with me forever; a truth that affects everything I do really, a realization found in sound and then confirmed among the gum trees sitting above the river in a park that makes you feel like you're in the outback. Did Adelaide's planners envision how potent this could all be when they set a huge ring of parks right around the city centre, creating a unique city plan? Who knows. The next day at Adelaide Airport, I saw Beach House and I told them what I now knew to be true, and that the show the previous night had illuminated something big to me. I wonder if they remember. Parks are truly the places where things happen.

HYDE PARK

Sydney, Australia

Numerous sights make Hyde Park worth a visit. The Hyde Park Barracks at the north-east corner is one of Australia's oldest architectural achievements, a once grimy hostel for convicts by the forger-turned-colony-architect Francis Greenway. Inside you can see the old hammocks swinging and wonder what life was like for the confused and homesick inmates straight off the boat. Museum and St James stations on the Sydney rail network are preserved in aspic as if it was a hundred years ago; I especially love the retro advertisements for Chateau Tanunda Brandy. Outside the latter is Metro, a cute little café-bar. Parts of the park are taken over for the Sydney Festival's annual shindigs, where you can witness ostentatiously avant-garde arts and eat gelato while you dodge the so-called 'bin chickens', the sinister-looking, black-beaked ibis. At the southern end of the formal park is a reflecting pool and a monument to the ANZAC soldiers.

EDINBURGH GARDENS

Melbourne, Australia

I found out for myself just how welcoming Aussies are when cousins of my friend laid on a genuine down-under barbecue for us all in Melbourne's most hipster park. They popped open slabs of Coopers Green Beer from the bottle-o and grilled kangaroo steaks, and I tasted the marsupial for the first time and made jokes about *Neighbours* and Ned Kelly they took in good spirits – before lamenting our (English) performance at the cricket. The public barbecues here and in almost every Aussie park speak to a strong sense of both community and gentle hedonism – they're always cared for and always popular. The park is a haven for Brunswick hipsters in black, dog walkers and Melbourne's multicultural masses. There's a bowling green where you can do your best Harold Bishop impression and usually plenty of good old Aussie rockers throwing around an Aussie Rules football too.

Pioneering
Women in Parks

Kate Wills

Author of *A Trip of One's Own: Hope,
Heartbreak and Why Travelling Solo
Could Change Your Life*

Tucked away in an unassuming corner of Victoria Park sits a
monument to one of the most interesting women in history.
Take a moment to read the plaque next to the gothic granite
drinking fountain by Hackney Gate and you'll discover Angela
Burdett-Coutts. Once known as the richest woman in England,
this Victorian philanthropist co-founded a home for prostitutes
with Charles Dickens, set up Columbia Road market, brought
drinking water to the East End and shocked the nation when she
married her 29-year-old male secretary. She was 67 at the time.

If you want to discover some of the UK's most pioneering
women, head to your nearest park. Although only 4 per cent of
the capital's public statues depict women (shockingly, London
has more statues of animals than it does women or people
of colour) they are nearly all to be found in the city's green
spaces. In nearby Shoreditch Park you'll find a memorial garden
for Dorothy Thurtle, who campaigned for women's rights to

birth control in the 1930s. Head to Mile End Park to find a steel sculpture of suffragette Sylvia Pankhurst. Stroll around Tavistock Square and say hello to writer Virginia Woolf, as well as Dame Louisa Aldrich-Blake, the first female surgeon, and in the adjacent Gordon Square find a statue of Noor Inayat Khan, an Indian princess who became a secret agent for the British in the Second World War, and whose incredible story is crying out for a Hollywood movie. In many ways it feels appropriate that so many of our green spaces celebrate and commemorate women. When parks and 'pleasure gardens' first opened in Britain they were seen, like shopping centres, as transitional places where women could safely 'promenade' in public.

I've certainly spent a lot of my life in parks over the last few years. Having my daughter Blake in the middle of the pandemic meant that my local park became the epicentre of my existence. Not since I was a teenager had I clocked up so many hours on scraggly patches of greenery, in all kinds of weather. I now feel like I know Victoria Park intimately, every bench, every tree, every browning patch of grass. I notice when new flowers sprout, when trees come into blossom and grow bare, and have watched both ducklings and newbie rollerskaters take flight. And I know all about extraordinary women such as Angela. So that's a bonus.

ALBERT PARK

Auckland, New Zealand

Stroll up from Shortland Street and, as you rise above the city, you can feel your head clear. Auckland's central, formal park is filled with city workers, young guns and students from the next-door university (brutalism fans: check out some of the uni's intriguing mid-century teaching and administration buildings). Naturally there's a statue of Queen Victoria to keep the British theme front and centre. But today's New Zealand is much more globalized – as is its horticulture. Though that tradition has been going for some time and the planting here is truly international in scope. There's the famous Argentine ombu tree at its centre: with its weird and wonderful roots and crazy crooked shape it is a favourite hangout and climbing spot. There are also Canary Island date palms, a Chinese maidenhair tree, an Indian bead tree, a South African Cape chestnut, an Irish yew and a Dutch elm, all feeling most at home in this sunny spot.

YARRA VALLEY PARKLANDS

Melbourne, Australia

Just to the east of Melbourne's city centre you'll find an abundance of parklands on each side of the River Yarra. The unifying theme here is sport. Yarra Parklands' lawns stretch out towards the famous Melbourne Cricket Ground (aka the 'G') – one of the world's biggest cricket stadiums, which hosts the annual Boxing Day Test match all Aussies sit around the TV watching and sweating over. Aussie Rules games are played here too; Richmond's home oval is in the park but they play in the 'G' sometimes. In fact, some of the first ever Australian Rules matches were played in this park. Cross the Yarra River and you find the Rod Laver Arena where the Australian Open Tennis is held. Close by is AAMI Park stadium, where rugby union's Rebels and rugby league's Storm play, as do Melbourne Victory and Melbourne City football (soccer) teams. In Alexandra Gardens there are various rowing clubs by the river and a skate park. You'll find plenty of runners and cyclists pounding the paved roads around Kings Domain and yoga taking place on the grass every morning (Aussies start early and do their exercise before brekkie, which is always avo toast, natch). It's enough to make you need a sit-down and a tinny.

COMMONWEALTH PARK

Canberra, Australia

Flower fans will love Floriade, the festival of blooms that brings Canberra's Commonwealth Park to life every September and October and is, in itself, one of the Australian capital's major attractions, drawing half a million visitors every year. Ask anyone who's grown up here with diplomatic or academic parents and they'll smile as they cast their mind back to school-age trips round the displays that kids seem to love. At any other time of the year you can enjoy the views across Lake Burley Griffin towards the National Library, National Museum of Art and High Court, all good, solid mid-century structures. There's also the Captain Cook Memorial Jet, which burps water 150 metres into the air along the park's shoreline, and plenty of art to explore as you walk the park, including a Barbara Hepworth. And there's the National Capital Exhibition – a great little museum which tells the story of Canberra's founding and planning.

BOTANIC GARDENS

Wellington, New Zealand

The genteel parklands of New Zealand's capital are set on a hill overlooking this most alluring of cities, where life seems always to be sweet (save for the wind and the vampires – if you haven't watched *What We Do in the Shadows*, you should). Take a cable car up to the top or go jogging like so many do in the early morning. Once inside there are plenty of things to see: artworks by Henry Moore and Denis O'Connor, the Carter Observatory looking at the planets, the Begonia House filled with exotic plants, and for rose fans the Lady Norwood Rose Garden. There are also set-piece planting zones featuring cacti, succulents and aloes, and plenty of coniferous tress to give shade during a picnic. The famous Peace Flame is a one-off – lit from the burning fires of Hiroshima after the nuclear bomb was dropped there in 1945, the flame was presented to the city by Japan in 1975 and stands as a stark reminder of the destruction of atomic weapons and of New Zealand's famous opposition to them.

FURTHER READING

Hunter Davies, *The Heath: My Year on Hampstead Heath* (Apollo, 2021)

Travis Elborough, *A Walk in the Park: The Life and Times of a People's Institution* (Jonathan Cape, 2016)

Gemma Reeves, *Victoria Park* (Allen & Unwin, 2021)

Parks and Recreation (NBC TV)

CAPTIONS FOR CHAPTER OPENERS

Pages 18-19: Holyrood Park, Edinburgh, Scotland

Pages 54-55: Parc de la Villette, Paris, France

Pages 98-99: Central Park, New York, USA

Pages 132-133: Zhishan Garden, Taipei, Taiwan

Pages 174-175: Alexandra Gardens, Melbourne, Australia

PICTURE CREDITS

ABOUT THE AUTHOR

Christopher Beanland is a comedy writer and the author of the novels *The Wall in the Head* and *Spinning Out of Control*. He's also written the non-fiction books *Unbuilt*, *Lido* and *Concrete Concept: Brutalist Buildings Around the World*, as well as numerous pieces of journalism. He lives in London.

Twitter: @chrisbeanland
Instagram: @christopherbeanland
Website: christopherbeanland.com

Listen to the comedy podcast Park Date in which Christopher interviews different people in different parks.
Twitter: @parkdatepodcast
Instagram: @parkdatepodcast
Website: parkdate.co.uk

CONTRIBUTORS

James Drury (pages 34-35): jamesdruryphotography.myportfolio.com/
Samantha Lewis (pages 52-53): @samlewis400
Travis Elborough (pages 70-73): traviselborough.co.uk
Harriet Thorpe (pages 92-33): www.htprojects.org
Andre D. L. McLeod (pages 150-151): @andredlmcleod
Kate Wills (pages 182-183): kate-wills.com

THANK YOU

Carole and John and Michael Beanland, Kate and Anna Beanland-Hall.
Zena Alkayat, Charlotte Gill, Nick Francis, Rowan and Lydia and Delilah Collinson,
Clare McQue, Roisin and Iona Inglesby, Therese Spruhan, Helen Coffey,
Felicity Cloake, Vicky Baker, Tim Gray, Lucy Smith, Ben Norris,
Hannah van der Westhuysen, Rosie Wilby, Sophia Ignatidou, Jazmin Burgess,
Alyx Gorman, Travis Elborough, Iain Sinclair, Chris Petit, Rowan Woods,
Tamsin Wressell, Martha Hayes, Catherine O'Flynn, Michael Cumming,
William Hanson, Chris Grimley, Lottie Flach, Ben Fisher, Brenna Johnston,
Sadie Venetia Whitelocks, Laura Frances Green, David Ellis, Simon Hawkins,
Cassie Ledger, Ross Purdie, Lexi Brown, Sophy Grimshaw, Barbara Speed,
Dan Fahey, Lauren Turner, Holly Frith, Beca Merriman, Hardeep Phull,
Deborah Arthurs, Kat Wagner, Alexandra Haddow, Matt Arnold, Freya Bromley,
Holly Fisher, Ben Olsen, Kirsty Major, Hugh Montgomery, David Ellis, Mark Thomas,
Shazia Mirza, Harriet Kemsley. Everyone at Batsford: Nicola Newman (greatest
editor), Frida Green (greatest PR), Gemma Doyle, Lilly Phelan, Tina Persaud.
Podcast experts: Mae-Li Evans, Lucia Scazzochio, Luke Jones, Clare Chadburn,
Mayana McDermott, Mike Adefuye.

Top hat wearer: David Baldwin.
Raya liaison officer: Andre McLeod.
Jacket potato marketing lead: Rebecca Lane.
"Let's hang by the canal": Andrew Trendell.
Burgers and butterflies: Raziq Rauf.
Stelfox appreciation society: James and Ashleigh Drury.
Chief vintage store finder: Sam Lewis.
Anthea Turner lookalike: Kat Squire.
Surrogate parents: Steve Pill, Ravneet Ahluwalia.
90s music choices: Lucy Bright.
Susie Steiner impersonations: Nicola Trup.

Special thanks to these amazing people who cheered up a dismal lockdown: Jo,
Lorna, Rachel, Rachel, Sophie, Alissa, Laura, Eliana, Liv, Annie, Madeleine, Francesca,
Harriet, Dr Sara, Dominika, Stine, Anna, Amy, Magda, Joanna, Andrea, Maria, Marie
Lou, Fernanda, Laura, Vivianna, Tabita, Cecile. You all helped to galvanize this book.

INDEX

Page references to illustrations are in *italics*.

Abney Park Cemetery, Stoke Newington, London 13
Adelaide, Australia 178, *179*
airports 60, 149
Albania: Grand Park, Tirana *84*, 85
Albert Park, Auckland *188*, 189, *190–1*
Aldrich-Blake, Louisa 187
Alexandra Gardens, Melbourne *174–5*
amphitheatres 88
Arnos Park, London 171
Arthur's Seat, Edinburgh *18–19*, 38, *39*
Assemble 171
Atlanta: Beltline 130
Atomium 94
Auckland: Albert Park *188*, 189, *190–1*
Augarten, Vienna *74*, 75
Australia
  Adelaide 178, *179*
  Alexandra Gardens, Melbourne *174–5*
  Barangaroo Reserve, Sydney *176*, 177
  Commonwealth Park, Canberra 194, *195*
  Edinburgh Gardens, Melbourne *184*, 185
  Goods Line, Sydney 130
  Hyde Park, Sydney *4–5*, 180, *181*, *182–3*
  Sydney Park, Australia *92–3*
  Yarra Valley Parklands, Melbourne *192*, 193
Austria
  Augarten, Vienna *74*, 75
  Schloss Belvedere, Vienna 74

Ballard, J. G. 149
bandstands 24, *179*
Bangkok: Lumphini Park 140, *141*
Banham, Reyner 11
Barangaroo Reserve, Sydney *176*, 177
Barcelona
  linear parks 93
  Park Güell *62*, 63, *64–5*
Barnsdall Art Park, Los Angeles 17
BBC Radio 1 Roadshow 37
The Beatles 72
Belfast: Botanic Gardens 28, *29–31*
Belgium: Heysel, Brussels 94, *95*
Beltline, Atlanta 130
benches 13, *63*, 70

Berlin
  Olympiapark 151
  Tempelhof 60, *61*
  Tiergarten 78, *79–81*
Birkenhead Park, Merseyside 11, 71, *72*
Birmingham
  Perry Park 37
  Sutton Park *36*, 37
Blatterwiese, Zürich *86*, 87
Bloomingdale Line, Chicago 130
Bofill, Ricardo 77
Bois de Vincennes, Paris 151
Bosque Urbano, Madrid 93
Boston
  Boston Common 11
  Rose Kennedy Greenway *118*, 119
Botanic Gardens, Belfast 28, *29–31*
Botanic Gardens, Wellington *196*, 197, *198–9*
Brazil
  Ibirapuera Park, São Paulo *104*, 105
  Minhocão, São Paulo 163
Brockwell Park, London 150
Brussels: Heysel 94, *95*
Buffalo: Riverline 130
Bunhill Fields, Islington, London 13
Burdett-Coutts, Angela 186
Burnham, Daniel 139

cable cars 173, *197*, *198–9*
Cahill, Kevin 14
Calatrava, Santiago 77
Camden High Line, London 130
Canada
  Mount Royal Park, Montreal 120, *121–3*
  Stanley Park, Vancouver *112*, 113
  Canberra: Commonwealth Park 194, *195*
Cape Town: Table Mountain Reserve *172*, 173
Cardiff: Linear Park 14–16
cemeteries 12, 13, 120
Central Park, New York 11, 53, 72, *98–9*, 110, *111*
Central Park, Taichung 93
Chelsea Flower Show *47*, 49–50
Chicago
  Bloomingdale Line 130
  Millennium Park and Grant Park *106*, 107, *108–9*

children 6, 8, 166–71
China
  Houtan Park, Shanghai 152, *153–5*
  Victoria Peak Garden, Hong Kong *156*, 157, *158–9*
  Xuhui Runway Park, Shanghai *148*, 149
Churchill Gardens, Pimlico, London *168–9*, 171
Cimetière du Père Lachaise, Paris 13
Clapham Common, London *150–1*
Clissold Park, London 14, 72
Cloud Gate (Kapoor) 107
Coe, Jonathan 94
Commonwealth Park, Canberra 194, *195*
concerts 33
Coram's Fields, Bloomsbury, London *170*, 171
cricket 193
Crystal Palace Park, London 44, *45*
Cyprus: Eleftheria Square, Nicosia 14, *15*
Czech Republic: Letna Gardens, Prague 35

deer 33
Derrida, Jacques 67
Dickens, Charles 186
Diller Scofidio + Renfro 96
dinosaur sculptures 44
Doha 50
Drury, James 34–5
Dublin: Phoenix Park *32*, 33
Durant, Sam 129–30
Düsseldorf: Hofgarten 7, *82*, 83

East Park, Hull 72
Edinburgh Gardens, Melbourne *184*, 185
Edinburgh: Holyrood Park and Arthur's Seat *18–19*, 38, *39*
Eisenman, Peter 67
Elborough, Travis 70–3
Eleftheria Square, Nicosia 14, *15*
English Gardens, Munich *68*, 69
exercise 52–3
exhibitions 44, 46, 87, 94, 152, 171

festivals
  garden festivals 46–50, *51*, 194
  music and arts 20, 107, *150–1*, 177, 178

Finsbury Park, London 14, 53
Flakturms 74
Floriade festivals, Netherlands 50
Folkestone Harbour Arm 128, 130
football stadiums/teams 24, 44, 94
'forest bathing' 53
Fort Canning Park, Singapore 142, 143-5
France
  Bois de Vincennes, Paris 151
  Cimetière du Père Lachaise, Paris 13
  Jardin des Tuileries, Paris 10, 11, 74
  La Promenade Plantée, Paris 124, 125
  Parc de la Villette, Paris 54-5, 66, 67
Freeway Park, Seattle 100, 101, 102-3

garden festivals 46-50, 51
gardens, private 9-11
Gateway Park, Rosslyn 101
Gaudí, Antoni 63
Gehry, Fank 107
Germany
  English Gardens, Munich 68, 69
  garden festivals 50, 51
  Hofgarten, Düsseldorf 7, 82, 83
  Olympiapark, Berlin 151
  Tempelhof, Berlin 60, 61
  Tiergarten, Berlin 78, 79-81
Glasgow
  garden festival 49
  Glasgow Green 151
  Glasgow Necropolis 13
Golden Gate Park, San Francisco 171
Goldfinger, Ernő 171
Goods Line, Sydney 130
Gordon Square, London 187
Grand Park, Tirana 84, 85
Grant Park, Chicago 106, 107, 108-9
Green Link, London 73
Griffith Park, Los Angeles 17, 114, 115-17
Güell, Eusebi 63
Guerrilla Gardeners 16

Hackney Downs, London 12
Hadid, Zaha 14
Haig, Matt 17
Halprin, Lawrence 101
Hampstead Heath and Primrose Hill, London 41, 42, 43-4
Hansaviertel, Berlin 78
Heaton Park, Manchester 151
Henry VIII 37
Hepworth, Barbara 194
Herzog, Werner 8, 9
Heysel, Brussels 94, 95
High Line, New York 73, 124, 126-7, 129-30

Hiroshima: Peace Memorial Park 12, 146, 147
history of parks 11-12, 70-3
Hofbogen, Rotterdam 130
Hofgarten, Düsseldorf 7, 82, 83
Holyrood Park and Arthur's Seat, Edinburgh 18-19, 38, 39
Hong Kong: Victoria Peak Garden 156, 157, 158-9
Houtan Park, Shanghai 152, 153-5
Hoxha, Enver 85
Hughes, Robert 105
Hull: East Park 72
human condition 8-9
Hyde Park, London 11
Hyde Park, Sydney 4-5, 180, 181, 182-3

Ibirapuera Park, São Paulo 104, 105
Indigenous People's Park, Taipei 160
Ireland: Phoenix Park, Dublin 32, 33

Japan
  Peace Memorial Park, Hiroshima 12, 146, 147
  Yoyogi Park & Meiji Jingu Shrine Park, Tokyo 35, 134, 135, 136-7
Jardin des Tuileries, Paris 10, 11, 74
Jephson Gardens, Leamington Spa 35
Jujol, Josep Maria 63

Kapoor, Anish 107
Keller Fountain Park, Oregon 101
Kensington Gardens, London 167
Khan, Noor Inayat 187
King's Lynn: The Walks 24, 25

La Promenade Plantée, Paris 124, 125
Lamas, Nicolas 57
Lanyon, Charles 28
Łazienki Park, Warsaw 88, 89-91
Le Corbusier 87
Leamington Spa: Jephson Gardens 35
Leeds: Woodhouse Moor 26, 27
Lennon, John 72
Letna Gardens, Prague 35
Lewis, Samantha 52-3
lidos 11-12, 20, 37
Linear Park, Cardiff 14-16
linear parks 73, 93, 152
Lisbon
  Parque da Bela Vista 151
  Parque Eduardo VII 56, 57, 58-9
Liverpool
  garden festival 48, 49
  Princes Park 11

London
  Abney Park Cemetery, Stoke Newington 13
  Arnos Park 171
  Brockwell Park, London 150
  Bunhill Fields, Islington 13
  Camden High Line 130
  Churchill Gardens, Pimlico 168-9, 171
  Clapham Common 150-1
  Clissold Park 14, 72
  Coram's Fields, Bloomsbury 170, 171
  Crystal Palace Park 44, 45
  Finsbury Park 14, 53
  Gordon Square 187
  Green Link 73
  Hackney Downs 12
  Hampstead Heath and Primrose Hill 41, 42, 43-4
  Hyde Park 11
  Kensington Gardens 167
  Marble Arch Mound 16-17
  Mile End Park 187
  Royal Parks 11
  St Mary Aldermanbury Garden 14
  Salters' Garden 14
  Shoreditch Park 186
  Southwark Park 73
  Springfield Park 72-3
  Tavistock Square 187
  Victoria Park 20, 21-3, 35, 70, 72, 150, 186, 187
  Wanstead Flats 34-5
Los Angeles
  Barnsdall Art Park 17
  Griffith Park 17, 114, 115-17
  Pershing Square 17
Love Parades 78
Low Line, New York 130
Lumphini Park, Bangkok 140, 141

McLeod, Andre D. L. 150-1
Madrid: Bosque Urbano 93
Manchester: Heaton Park 151
Manila: Rizal Park 138, 139
Marble Arch Mound, London 16-17
Marcos, Imelda 139
Marx, Roberto Burle 105
mazes 44
Meiji Jingu Shrine Park, Tokyo 35, 134, 135, 136-7
Melbourne
  Alexandra Gardens 174-5
  Edinburgh Gardens 184, 185
  Yarra Valley Parklands 192, 193
memorials 12, 70, 146, 147, 181
Merseyside: Birkenhead Park 11, 71, 72
Miami: The Underline 130, 131
Mile End Park, London 187

Millennium Park and Grant Park, Chicago 106, 107, 108–9
Minhocão, São Paulo 163
Minton, Anna 14
Miyawaki method 93
modernism 11, 46, 78, 135, 146, 171
Montreal: Mount Royal Park 120, 121–3
Moore, Henry 197
Moscow: Zaryadye Park 96, 97
Mount Royal Park, Montreal 120, 121–3
Mozart, Wolfgang Amadeus 74
Muir, John 9
Munich: English Gardens 68, 69
MVRDV 163

Nairn, Ian 11
Nash, Jacob 177
Netherlands
    Floriade festivals 50
    Hofbogen, Rotterdam 130
New York
    Central Park 11, 53, 72, 98–9, 110, 111
    High Line 73, 124, 126–7, 129–30
    Low Line 130
    Prospect Park, Brooklyn 35
New Zealand
    Albert Park, Auckland 188, 189, 190–1
    Botanic Gardens, Wellington 196, 197, 198–9
Nicosia: Eleftheria Square 14, 15
Niemeyer, Oscar 105
Nietzsche, Friedrich 14
Northern Ireland: Botanic Gardens, Belfast 28, 29–31
nuclear weapons 146, 197

observatories 114, 197
O'Connor, Denis 197
Olmstead, Frederick Law 11, 72, 120
Olympiapark, Berlin 151
One Big Weekend 37
Oregon: Keller Fountain Park 101

Pankhurst, Sylvia 187
Parc de la Villette, Paris 54–5, 66, 67
Paris
    Bois de Vincennes 151
    Cimetière du Père Lachaise 13
    Jardin des Tuileries 10, 11, 74
    La Promenade Plantée 124, 125
    Parc de la Villette 54–5, 66, 67
Park Güell, Barcelona 62, 63, 64–5
parklets 16
Parks and Recreation 11
Parque da Bela Vista, Lisbon 151
Parque Eduardo VII, Lisbon 56, 57, 58–9
Paxton, Joseph 44, 72

Peace Flame, Botanic Gardens, Wellington 197
Peace Memorial Park, Hiroshima 12, 146, 147
Perry Park, Birmingham 37
Pershing Square, Los Angeles 17
Philadelphia: Rail Park 130
Philippines: Rizal Park, Manila 138, 139
Phoenix Park, Dublin 32, 33
photography 34–5
Pierre, DBC 60
play/playgrounds 6, 166–71
Poehler, Amy 11
Poland: Łazienki Park, Warsaw 88, 89–91
popes 139
Portugal
    Parque da Bela Vista, Lisbon 151
    Parque Eduardo VII, Lisbon 56, 57, 58–9
Powell & Moya 171
Prague: Letna Gardens 35
Primrose Hill, London 41, 42, 43–4
Princes Park, Liverpool 11
private parks 13–14
Prospect Park, Brooklyn, New York 35

Qatar 50

Radio 1 Roadshow 37
Raffles, Stamford 142
Rail Park, Philadelphia 130
railways 37, 44, 113, 124, 129, 181
Reeves, Gemma 20
rewilding 93
riverbeds 77
Riverline, Buffalo 130
Rizal Park, Manila 138, 139
rockeries 72
Rose Kennedy Greenway, Boston 118, 119
Rosslyn: Gateway Park 101
Rotterdam: Hofbogen 130
Royal Horticultural Society 50
Royal Parks, London 11
Russia: Zaryadye Park, Moscow 96, 97

St Mary Aldermanbury Garden, London 14
Salters' Garden, London 14
San Francisco: Golden Gate Park 171
São Paulo
    Ibirapuera Park 104, 105
    Minhocão 163
Sasaki Architects 149
Schloss Belvedere, Vienna 74

Scotland
    Glasgow Green 151
    Glasgow Necropolis 13
    Holyrood Park and Arthur's Seat, Edinburgh 38, 39
sculpture 20, 44, 57, 107, 129–30, 194
Seattle: Freeway Park 100, 101, 102–3
Senna, Ayrton 105
Seoullo 7017, Seoul 162, 163, 164–5
Shanghai
    Houtan Park 152, 153–5
    Xuhui Runway Park 148, 149
Sheffield 73
shinrin-yoku 53
Shoreditch Park, London 186
Simpsons 124
Singapore: Fort Canning Park 142, 143–5
South Africa: Table Mountain Reserve, Cape Town 172, 173
South Korea: Seoullo 7017, Seoul 162, 163, 164–5
Southwark Park, London 73
Spain
    Bosque Urbano, Madrid 93
    Park Güell, Barcelona 62, 63, 64–5
    Turia Riverbed, Valencia 76, 77
'sponge city' 92, 149
Spratt, Vicky 14
Springfield Park, London 72–3
Stanley Park, Vancouver 112, 113
students 27
Succession 129
surfing 69
sustainability 92–3
Sutton Park, Birmingham 36, 37
Switzerland: Blatterwiese, Zürich 86, 87
Sydney
    Barangaroo Reserve 176, 177
    Goods Line 130
    Hyde Park 4–5, 180, 181, 182–3
    Sydney Park 92–3

Table Mountain Reserve, Cape Town 172, 173
Taiwan
    Central Park, Taichung 93
    Zhishan Gardens and Indigenous People's Park, Taipei 132–3, 160, 161
Tange, Kenzo 135, 146
Tavistock Square, London 187
Tempelhof, Berlin 60, 61
Terrill, Simon 171
Thailand: Lumphini Park, Bangkok 140, 141
Thorpe, Harriet 92–3
Thurtle, Dorothy 186–7

Tiergarten, Berlin 78, _79-81_
Tirana: Grand Park _84,_ 85
Tokyo: Yoyogi Park & Meiji Jingu
 Shrine Park 35, _134, 135, 136-7_
trams 157
Turenscape 152
Turia Riverbed, Valencia _76, 77_

UK see _also_ London
 Birkenhead Park, Merseyside 11, _71,_
 72
 Botanic Gardens, Belfast 28, _29-31_
 East Park, Hull 72
 Folkestone Harbour Arm _128,_ 130
 Glasgow Green 151
 Glasgow Necropolis 13
 Heaton Park, Manchester 151
 Holyrood Park and Arthur's Seat,
 Edinburgh _18-19,_ 38, 39
 Jephson Gardens, Leamington Spa
 35
 Perry Park, Birmingham 37
 Princes Park, Liverpool 11
 Sheffield 73
 Sutton Park, Birmingham 36, 37
 The Walks, King's Lynn 24, 25
 Woodhouse Moor, Leeds 26, 27
 Yorkshire Sculpture Park 107
The Underline, Miami 130, _131_
USA
 Barnsdall Art Park, Los Angeles 17
 Beltline, Atlanta 130
 Bloomingdale Line, Chicago 130
 Boston Common, Boston 11
 Central Park, New York 11, 53, 72,
 _98-9,_ 110, _111_
 Freeway Park, Seattle _100,_ 101, _102-3_
 Gateway Park, Rosslyn 101
 Golden Gate Park, San Francisco
 171
 Griffith Park, Los Angeles 17, 114,
 _115-17_
 High Line, New York 73, 124, _126-7,_
 _129-_30
 Keller Fountain Park, Oregon 101
 Low Line, New York 130
 Millennium Park and Grant Park,
 Chicago _106,_ 107, _108-9_
 Pershing Square, Los Angeles 17
 Prospect Park, Brooklyn, New York
 35
 Rail Park, Philadelphia 130
 Riverline, Buffalo 130
 Rose Kennedy Greenway, Boston
 _118,_ 119
 The Underline, Miami 130, _131_

Valencia: Turia Riverbed _76, 77_

Vancouver: Stanley Park _112,_ 113
Vaux, Calvert 72
Victoria Park, London 20, _21-3,_ 35, 70,
 72, 150, 186, 187
Victoria Peak Garden, Hong Kong
 156, 157, _158-9_
Vienna
 Augarten _74,_ 75
 Schloss Belvedere 74

Wales: Linear Park, Cardiff _14-16_
The Walks, King's Lynn: King's Lynn
 24, 25
Wanstead Flats, London _34-5_
Warsaw: Łazienki Park 88, _89-91_
Wellington: Botanic Gardens _196,_ 197,
 _198-9_
wellness _52-3_
Weyhe, Maximilian 82
wildness 93
Wills, Kate _186-7_
women _186-7_
Woodhouse Moor, Leeds 26, 27
Woolf, Virginia 187

Xuhui Runway Park, Shanghai _148,_ 149

Yarra Valley Parklands, Melbourne
 _192,_ 193
yoga _52-3_
Yorkshire Sculpture Park 107
Yoyogi Park & Meiji Jingu Shrine Park,
 Tokyo 35, _134, 135, 136-7_

Zaryadye Park, Moscow 96, 97
Zhishan Gardens and Indigenous
 People's Park, Taipei _132-3, 160, 161_
Zürich: Blatterwiese 86, 87